Unlocking Potential: A Guide to Valid Recognition of Prior Learning (RPL)

Dr. Francois Meyer (DTh, DD, PhD)

Published by Dr. Francois Meyer (DTh, DD, PhD), 2024.

While every precaution has been taken in the preparation of this book, the publisher assumes no responsibility for errors or omissions, or for damages resulting from the use of the information contained herein.

UNLOCKING POTENTIAL: A GUIDE TO VALID RECOGNITION OF PRIOR LEARNING (RPL)

First edition. April 26, 2024.

Copyright © 2024 Dr. Francois Meyer (DTh, DD, PhD).

ISBN: 979-8224150762

Written by Dr. Francois Meyer (DTh, DD, PhD).

Introduction:

Lifelong learning has become essential for personal and professional growth, and the model of Recognition of Prior Learning (RPL) has emerged as a vital tool for individuals seeking to validate their existing knowledge and skills. This book is a comprehensive guide to understanding and implementing valid RPL practices, catering to assessors, moderators, subject matter experts, students, and potential RPL candidates.

By recognizing prior learning, we acknowledge that individuals acquire valuable skills and knowledge through various formal, non-formal, and informal learning experiences outside traditional educational settings. By using these experiences, RPL offers individuals the opportunity to gain formal recognition for their competencies, facilitating access to further education, career advancement, and lifelong learning pathways.

The need for validity is the centre of RPL, and ensures that the assessment processes and outcomes are fair, reliable, and credible.

It is extremely important for assessors and moderators to understand how to conduct valid RPL assessments. It involves critically evaluating evidence provided by candidates to determine its relevance, authenticity, and sufficiency in meeting the requirements of specific qualifications or standards.

Additionally, Subject Matter Experts play a crucial role in RPL, providing valuable insights into industry-relevant competencies and standards. Their expertise helps align RPL assessments with current industry practices, ensuring that candidates are evaluated against meaningful and applicable criteria.

For students and potential RPL candidates, the importance of understanding valid RPL practices cannot be overstated. It empowers them to navigate the RPL process confidently, knowing what evidence to gather, how to present it effectively, and what to expect from the assessment process. By understanding RPL and promoting transparency, individuals can make informed decisions about their learning pathways and future career prospects.

In this book, we explore the details of valid RPL practices, offering practical guidance, case studies, and insights from industry experts. We examine the principles of Validity, Authenticity, Reliability, Currency, and Sufficiency (VARCS) in RPL assessment, emphasizing their importance in upholding the integrity and credibility of the process.

Additionally, we provide comprehensive resources and tools for assessors, moderators, and subject matter experts to enhance their understanding and implementation of valid RPL practices. From developing assessment criteria to conducting evidence evaluations, this book equips professionals with the knowledge and skills needed to facilitate fair and effective RPL assessments.

Our goal is to promote a culture of lifelong learning and recognition, where individuals can unite and use their diverse experiences and talents ad stepping stones to achieve their educational and career aspirations. By embracing valid RPL practices, we can unlock the potential of learners, empower professionals, and create pathways to success for all.

Chapter 1

Introduction to Recognition of Prior Learning (RPL)

What is RPL?

What exactly is Recognition of Prior Learning (RPL)?

It is an excellent opportunity for individuals to demonstrate their abilities and expertise, regardless of how or where they learned it. RPL highlights the valuable knowledge and skills that frequently remain unnoticed in conventional educational environments.

Imagine dedicating years to refining your skills in a specific field, addressing real-world issues, and mastering various competencies. Now, what if you can turn these rich experiences into formal credentials? That is precisely the opportunity that RPL offers.

RPL acknowledges that learning is not confined to classrooms or structured training programs. It values experiential learning, understanding that skills and knowledge can be acquired through work experience, volunteering, self-learning, hobbies, and other non-traditional avenues.

RPL is about giving credit where credit is due. It recognizes the full spectrum of an individual's life-long learning journey; from the formal qualifications they have obtained, to the practical skills they have developed through hands-on experience. By acknowledging and valuing this prior learning, RPL opens doors to further education, career advancement, and personal growth that might otherwise remain closed.

One of the key principles of RPL is that everyone has something valuable to contribute. Whether you are a seasoned professional with decades of experience or someone just starting their career journey, RPL ensures that your skills and knowledge are given the recognition they deserve.

Now, you might be wondering, "How does RPL really work in practice?"

It typically involves a structured assessment process where individuals can provide evidence of their prior learning to demonstrate their competence in a particular subject or skill area. This evidence could take many forms, including work samples, portfolios, references from employers or colleagues, certifications, or even practical demonstrations of skills.

Once the evidence has been submitted, trained assessors evaluate it against established criteria to determine whether the individual meets the requirements for formal recognition. This assessment process is rigorous and fair, ensuring that individuals are given credit only for the skills and knowledge they can genuinely demonstrate.

RPL is not just about getting a badge for what you already know. It is also a pathway to further learning and development. For example, if you are seeking admission to a university program or professional certification, RPL can help you bypass redundant coursework and focus on areas where you still have room to grow.

Recognition of Prior Learning (RPL) offers a transformative opportunity for people of all ages and backgrounds. It allows you to go beyond the limitations of traditional education and show your true abilities. Whether you are an experienced professional looking to validate your skills or someone starting a new career path, RPL provides a pathway to recognition, advancement, and endless possibilities.

Importance of RPL in Education and Workforce Development.

Why does Recognition of Prior Learning (RPL) matter?

RPL transforms the way we approach education and career development, where your previous experiences and skills are valued and acknowledged.

What about education?
Traditional education systems have long been criticized for their one-size-fits-all approach, where learners are expected to follow a predetermined curriculum, regardless of their existing skills or knowledge. This approach often leads to frustration and disengagement, especially among adult learners who bring a wealth of life experience to the table.

RPL is the ultimate solution to standardized education. By recognizing and valuing prior learning, RPL offers a more personalized and flexible approach to education that honours the diverse pathways individuals take to acquire knowledge and skills. RPL allows you to bypass unnecessary coursework and focus on areas where you still have room to grow.

But RPL is not just about empowering individual learners, it is also about meeting the evolving needs of the workforce. In today's ever-changing job market, employers are constantly seeking workers with the right mix of skills and competencies to drive innovation and growth. Yet, traditional hiring practices often overlook the valuable skills and knowledge individuals bring from their past experiences.

That is where RPL changes workforce development. By recognizing and accrediting the skills individuals have acquired through work experience, volunteering, or other non-formal learning settings, RPL helps bridge the gap between the skills workers possess and the skills that employers demand. This not only benefits individual workers by enhancing their employability and career prospects, but also strengthens the overall competitiveness and productivity of the workforce.

Imagine you are hiring for a top job at your company. You have two candidates: one with lots of hands-on experience in leading teams and running projects, and the other with only book knowledge. Who would you pick? You would probably choose the one with real-world skills. That is where RPL helps by showing what people can really do. By providing a formal mechanism for recognizing and validating prior learning, RPL helps employers identify talent more effectively and make informed hiring decisions. It also encourages lifelong learning and professional development among employees, as they see their skills and achievements recognized and rewarded.

RPL benefits not only individual learners and employers but also educational institutions themselves. By embracing RPL practices, institutions can attract a more diverse range of learners and enhance their reputation as learner-centred institutions committed to recognizing and nurturing the full spectrum of learners' abilities.

But perhaps the most significant impact of RPL is its potential to break down barriers to education and employment, particularly for marginalized groups and disadvantaged communities. By recognizing the skills and knowledge individuals already possess, regardless of how or where they acquired them, RPL promotes inclusivity and equity in education and workforce development, creating opportunities for all to succeed.

The importance of RPL in education and workforce development cannot be overstated. It's a motivation for change, empowering individuals to unlock their full potential, helping employers identify and harness talent more effectively, and driving innovation and growth in the global economy. So, whether you're a learner, an employer, or an educational institution, embracing RPL is not just a smart move, it is a game-changer that can transform lives and communities for the better.

Formal recognition in Recognition of Prior Learning (RPL)

Formal recognition in Recognition of Prior Learning (RPL) refers to the official acknowledgment and validation of an individual's existing skills, knowledge, and competencies acquired through various formal learning experiences, such as previous education, training, work experience, or other life experiences.

In RPL processes, formal recognition involves assessing and evaluating an individual's prior learning against established standards or qualifications. This assessment is typically carried out by qualified assessors, or assessors who are knowledgeable in the relevant field or industry. If the assessment determines that the individual meets the required standards or competencies, they are granted formal recognition, which may include academic credits, qualifications, or certifications without having to undergo formal training or education for those specific skills or knowledge areas again.

Formal recognition in RPL is valuable, because it allows individuals to receive credit for their existing skills and knowledge, thereby saving time and resources by avoiding unneeded training or education. It also promotes lifelong learning and enables individuals to progress in their careers or pursue further education based on their existing competencies.

Formal recognition in Recognition of Prior Learning (RPL) often includes the awarding of formal qualifications such as accredited certificates, diplomas, or degrees. When an individual's prior learning is assessed and found to meet the required standards or competencies of a particular qualification, they are typically awarded the corresponding formal credential.

For example, if someone has acquired relevant skills and knowledge through work experience, self-study, or informal training that align with the requirements of a specific certification or diploma program, they may undergo an RPL assessment. If the assessment confirms that their prior learning meets the standards set for the qualification, they can be awarded the formal qualification without having to complete the entire formal training program.

Formal qualifications obtained through RPL are usually recognized by educational institutions, employers, and relevant regulatory bodies, making them valuable assets for individuals seeking career advancement or further education opportunities.

Benefits of RPL for Learners and Institutions

RPL can boost your educational journey or institution.

It is about empowering individuals to achieve their full potential.

So, what is in it for you as a learner?

RPL is a fast-track to success.

Imagine that you have spent years working in a particular industry, perfecting your skills, solving real-world problems, and climbing the career ladder. Now, imagine being able to translate those years of hard work and experience into formal recognition. That is exactly what RPL allows you to do. By recognizing and accrediting your prior learning, RPL can help you bypass redundant coursework and earn credits towards your educational goals quicker.

But that is just a small part thereof. RPL also opens doors to new opportunities and career pathways that may have been previously out of reach. Whether you are looking to switch careers, advance in your current field, or pursue further education, RPL can give you the competitive edge you need to stand out in a crowded job market. Employers appreciate candidates who can start working effectively right away, and RPL helps you stand out by highlighting your practical skills and abilities.

RPL is not just about rewarding for what you already know. It is also a pathway to further learning and personal growth. By recognizing your existing skills and knowledge, RPL allows you to focus your efforts on areas where you still have room to grow, whether it is through additional coursework, training, or hands-on experience. In other words, RPL puts you in control of your educational journey, allowing you to tailor your learning experiences to your individual needs and goals.

The benefits of RPL for institutions

Institutions can also benefit greatly from adopting RPL practices. Whether you are a university, college, training provider, or employer, RPL can be a paradigm shift and a major boost for your organization in more ways than one.

RPL can help institutions attract and retain a more diverse group of learners. Traditional education can be hard to access for adults or those from different backgrounds. RPL helps by recognizing and valuing the skills people have gained from past experiences, no matter how they learned them. This makes educational institutions more inclusive and shows that they care about meeting the needs of all learners.

RPL can enhance institutional efficiency and effectiveness. By streamlining the assessment process and leveraging existing resources, RPL allows institutions to save time and money while still ensuring accurate and high-quality assessment outcomes. This means fewer unneeded courses for the individual, faster time to completion, and more satisfied learners, a win-win for everyone involved.

RPL can also help institutions set the pace in a rapidly changing educational landscape. With the rise of online learning, competency-based education, and alternative credentialing options, RPL provides a flexible and adaptable framework for recognizing learning whenever and wherever it occurs. This allows institutions to stay relevant and responsive to the evolving needs of learners and employers, positioning them as leaders in educational innovation and excellence.

But perhaps the most significant benefit of RPL for institutions is the potential to drive institutional excellence and continuous improvement. By embracing RPL practices, institutions can promote a culture of lifelong learning and professional development among both staff and learners, promoting innovation, partnership, teamwork, and excellence across the board.

The benefits of Recognition of Prior Learning for both learners and institutions are clear and undeniable. From empowering individuals to achieve their educational and career goals to helping institutions attract, keep, and develop talent, RPL has the power to transform lives and communities for the better. So, whether you are a learner ready and excited to unlock your full potential, or an institution looking to stay ahead of the curve, embracing RPL is the obvious choice. The possibilities are endless, and the journey begins now.

Chapter 2

Understanding the RPL Process

In this chapter, we focus on the Recognition of Prior Learning (RPL) process.

and understanding how the process works is important to making the most of its benefits.

Overview of the RPL Assessment Process

First, we must look at what the RPL assessment process involves.

RPL is a systematic and structured process for assessing and accrediting an individual's prior learning. It is about recognizing and valuing the skills and knowledge individuals have acquired through work experience, volunteering, self-study, or other non-formal learning experiences.

The RPL assessment process typically involves several key steps:

** Initial Consultation:*

The process usually begins with an initial consultation between the learner and a trained RPL assessor or advisor. During this consultation, the learner will have the opportunity to discuss their goals, experiences, and aspirations, as well as the requirements and expectations of the RPL process.

Self-Assessment:

Next, the learner will engage in a process of self-assessment, where they reflect on their prior learning experiences and identify the skills, knowledge, and competencies they have acquired. This self-assessment helps the learner articulate their learning journey and prepare for the formal assessment process.

Gathering Evidence:

Once the self-assessment is complete, the learner will begin gathering evidence to support their claims of prior learning. This evidence could take many forms, including work samples, portfolios, certificates, references, or even practical demonstrations of skills.

Submission of Evidence:

Once the evidence has been gathered, the learner will submit it to the RPL assessor for evaluation. The assessor will review the evidence against established criteria to determine whether the learner meets the requirements for formal recognition.

Assessment and Feedback:

The assessor will then conduct an accurate and fair assessment of the evidence, providing constructive feedback to the learner along the way. This feedback is important and necessary for helping the learners understand their strengths and weaknesses and identify areas for further development.

Decision and Recognition:

Finally, based on the assessment findings, the assessor will decide whether the learner is suitable for RPL. If the learners meet the requirements, they will be formally recognized for their prior learning through the award of credits, qualifications, or other forms of recognition.

What is Established Criteria?

In the paragraph on 'submission of evidence', I mentioned that 'the assessor will review the evidence against established criteria'. To fully understand the meaning thereof, we must understand what established criteria is.

"Established criteria" in the context of Recognition of Prior Learning (RPL) refers to the predetermined standards or benchmarks used to assess and evaluate an individual's prior learning experiences. Think of it as the criteria or standard against which someone's knowledge, skills, and competencies are compared to, to determine if they meet the requirements for academic credit, certification, or other forms of recognition.

Imagine you have been working in the field of graphic design for several years but never pursued formal education in the subject. Now you are considering enrolling in a graphic design program at a university, but you don't want to start from scratch and attend full courses on the skills you already have. This is where RPL comes in. The university may have established criteria in place, outlining the requirements and outcomes to be met to be proficient in graphic design skills. These criteria could include things like knowledge of design principles, proficiency in industry-standard software, and a portfolio showcasing your work.

So, when you apply for RPL, the university will evaluate your prior learning against these established criteria. If your experience and skills align with what the university expects from its students, you may be granted credit for certain courses or even exempted from specific requirements, allowing you to fast-track your academic journey.

The criteria are predetermined and transparent, providing a clear framework for assessing prior learning. This ensures fairness and consistency in the evaluation process. Without established criteria, RPL assessments could be subjective and random, making it difficult for individuals to understand why they do or do not receive recognition for their prior learning.

Non-formal Training vs Informal Training

Before we proceed, it is important to understand the difference between the two. Non-formal and informal training are two distinct approaches to learning that differ in structure, context, and purpose.

Non-formal training

This is organized educational activities that take place outside the traditional formal education system. These activities are often structured and intentional, designed to teach specific skills or knowledge to learners. Non-formal training programs may be offered by institutions, community organizations, or employers and typically have defined objectives and outcomes. Examples include workshops, seminars, vocational training, and continuing education programs, Like CPD (Continuous Professional Development). Non-formal training often targets specific groups or populations and may be tailored to meet their needs and interests.

Informal training

This type of training is more spontaneous and unstructured. It occurs through daily life experiences and interactions rather than through planned instruction. Informal training can take place anywhere, such as on the job, at home, or in social settings, and is often driven by the learner's curiosity or immediate needs. It may involve observing others, trial and error, mentoring, or self-directed learning. Unlike non-formal training, informal training lacks a clear curriculum or assessment mechanism.

So, non-formal training is structured, intentional, and organized, while informal training is spontaneous, unstructured, and occurs naturally through everyday experiences. Both approaches play important roles in lifelong learning and skills development.

Overview of the RPL Assessment Process

The RPL assessment process is all about evaluating and validating the skills and knowledge individuals have acquired through non-formal and informal learning experiences. It is about recognizing that learning doesn't just happen in classrooms or through formal training programs but can occur anywhere and at any time.

So, how does the RPL assessment process work?

It typically involves several key steps, each designed to ensure a fair, accurate, and transparent assessment of an individual's prior learning.

** Initial Inquiry and Information Gathering:*

The RPL journey often begins with an individual expressing interest in pursuing RPL assessment. This could be a learner looking to gain recognition for their skills and knowledge or an employer seeking to assess the competencies of their workforce. During this initial inquiry stage, the individual is provided with information about the RPL process, including suitability criteria, evidence requirements, and assessment procedures.

** Self-Assessment and Documentation:*

Once the individuals decide to proceed with RPL assessment, they are typically asked to conduct a self-assessment of their prior learning. This involves reflecting on their experiences, skills, and knowledge and identifying relevant evidence to support their claims. This evidence could take various forms, including work samples, certificates, transcripts, references, and portfolios.

** Submission of Evidence:*

When the self-assessment is complete, the individuals gather and submit their evidence to the designated RPL assessor or assessment panel. This evidence forms the basis for the assessment, and provides the assessor(s) with a comprehensive overview of the individual's prior learning and competencies.

Assessment and Evaluation:

Once the evidence is submitted, the RPL assessor(s) carefully review and evaluate it against established criteria or standards. This assessment process may involve various methods, including interviews, observations, written assessments, and practical demonstrations, depending on the nature of the evidence and the requirements of the qualification or certification being sought.

Feedback and Decision Making:

After the assessment, the individuals receive feedback on their performance and the outcome of the assessment. This feedback may include strengths, areas for improvement, and recommendations for further learning or development. Based on the evidence presented and the assessment outcomes, a decision is made regarding whether the individual meets the requirements for RPL and is eligible for formal recognition.

Formal Recognition:

If the individuals successfully demonstrate their competence through the RPL assessment process, they are granted formal recognition of their prior learning. This recognition could take various forms, including credits towards a qualification, exemptions from certain courses or modules, or the awarding of a full qualification or certification.

Appeals and Review:

If the individuals disagree with the outcome of the assessment, they have the right to appeal the decision and request a review of the assessment process. This ensures that the RPL process remains fair, transparent, and accountable, with mechanisms in place to address any concerns or grievances.

Chapter 3

Legal and Ethical Considerations in RPL

Now that we have covered the basic steps of the RPL assessment process, we discuss the roles and responsibilities of the various stakeholders involved.

In any RPL assessment, there are three primary stakeholders:
* The learner,
* The assessor(s), and
* The institution.

Each one plays an important role in ensuring the success and integrity of the RPL process, so let's take a closer look at what each of these roles involves.

But before we do that, we must briefly discuss some key legal and ethical considerations that support and reinforce the RPL process. After all, integrity and fairness are the core of RPL, and it is essential to uphold these principles throughout the assessment journey. So, we need to understand the basics of the legal and ethical requirements of RPL before discussing the roles and responsibilities of stakeholders.

Legal and Ethical Considerations in RPL
What are the legal and ethical considerations in the RPL process?

While RPL offers many benefits, it is essential to ensure that the process is conducted in a manner that upholds the rights and interests of all parties involved.

From a legal perspective, institutions must ensure that their RPL policies and procedures comply with relevant legislation and regulatory requirements. This may include laws governing education, employment, privacy, equal opportunity, and human rights. Institutions must also ensure that their assessment practices are fair, transparent, and non-discriminatory, and that they provide appropriate mechanisms for addressing complaints and grievances.

From an ethical perspective, assessors must adhere to professional standards of conduct and integrity in their interactions with learners. This includes treating learners with respect and dignity, maintaining confidentiality and privacy, avoiding conflicts of interest, and providing honest and impartial feedback. Assessors must also ensure that their assessments are based on reliable and valid evidence and that they make decisions that are in the best interests of the learner and the institution.

Understanding the RPL process, roles, and responsibilities of stakeholders, and legal and ethical considerations is essential for ensuring the integrity and effectiveness of the RPL process. By adhering to best practices and principles, institutions can embrace the full potential of RPL to empower learners, enhance workforce development, and promote lifelong learning and professional development.

It is important to emphasize t the legal and ethical principles or RPL, as it is these foundational standards that strengthen the integrity, fairness, and validity of the assessment process.

Legal Considerations:

When it comes to RPL, legal considerations are highly important, ensuring that the assessment process adheres to relevant laws, regulations, and standards. Here are some key legal considerations to keep in mind:

** Equal Opportunity and Anti-Discrimination Laws:*
    One of the foundational principles of RPL is equal opportunity, ensuring that all individuals have impartial and unbiased access to RPL assessment regardless of their background, characteristics, or circumstances. It is essential to comply with anti-discrimination laws and regulations that prohibit discrimination based on race, gender, age, disability, or other protected characteristics.

** Data Protection and Privacy Laws:*
    In the digital age, safeguarding personal data and respecting the privacy rights of individuals is more important than ever. When collecting, storing, and processing personal information as part of the RPL assessment process, it is crucial to comply with data protection and privacy laws, such as the General Data Protection Regulation (GDPR) in the European Union, or the Health Insurance Portability

and Accountability Act (HIPAA) in the United States, and the Protection of Personal Information Act (POPIA) in South Africa.

** Intellectual Property Rights:*

Intellectual property rights, including copyrights, trademarks, and patents, must be respected, and protected throughout the RPL assessment process. This includes ensuring that learners' work samples, portfolios, and other evidence are used and assessed in accordance with applicable copyright laws and regulations.

** Contractual Obligations:*

In some cases, institutions may enter into contractual agreements with learners, assessors, or third-party providers regarding the provision of RPL assessment services. It is essential to uphold the terms and conditions of these contracts and ensure that all parties fulfil their obligations in good faith.

** Quality Assurance and Accreditation Requirements:*

Depending on the jurisdiction and the nature of the qualifications or certifications being sought, RPL assessments may need to meet certain quality assurance and accreditation standards set forth by relevant regulatory bodies or accrediting agencies. It is very important to ensure compliance with these requirements to maintain the integrity and credibility of the RPL process.

Ethical Considerations:

In addition to legal considerations, ethical principles guide the conduct of all stakeholders involved in the RPL process, ensuring fairness, transparency, and accountability.

Here are some important ethical considerations to consider:

Fairness and Equity:

The RPL process must be fair, unbiased, and impartial, providing all learners with an equal opportunity to demonstrate their skills and knowledge for assessment. This includes ensuring that assessment criteria are transparent, objective, and applied consistently to all learners, regardless of their background or circumstances.

Integrity and Honesty:

Integrity is the foundation of the RPL process, requiring all stakeholders to always act honestly, ethically, and transparently. This includes accurately representing one's skills and knowledge during the assessment process and refraining from any form of academic dishonesty or misconduct.

Respect for Diversity and Inclusion:

RPL must be open to diversity and should recognize the unique skills and experiences individuals bring from diverse backgrounds and cultures. It is essential to respect and value this diversity throughout the assessment process, avoiding stereotypes, biases, or assumptions based on race, gender, ethnicity, or other factors.

Confidentiality and Privacy:

Learners' personal information and assessment outcomes must be treated with the utmost confidentiality and privacy, in accordance with relevant data protection laws and ethical standards. This includes safeguarding sensitive information from unauthorized access, disclosure, or misuse.

Professionalism and Competence:

Assessors and other stakeholders involved in the RPL process must demonstrate professionalism, competence, and accountability in their roles. This includes maintaining up-to-date knowledge and skills relevant to RPL assessment, adhering to professional codes of conduct and ethics, and seeking guidance or support when needed.

Stakeholders must follow these legal and ethical considerations to ensure that the RPL process upholds the highest standards of integrity, fairness, and credibility. These principles strengthen the trust and confidence individuals place in the RPL process.

Chapter 4

The Necessity of Comparing RPL Evidence Against Unit Standards and Qualifications

Recognition of Prior Learning (RPL) is a valuable process that allows individuals to gain recognition for their existing skills and knowledge, regardless of how or where they were acquired. However, to ensure the credibility and validity of RPL outcomes, it is essential to compare the evidence provided by learners against established Unit Standards, part qualifications, or full qualifications provided by Qualifications Authorities. This chapter explores the necessity of this comparison process and its significance in confirming the skill and knowledge claimed through RPL.

Understanding the Importance of Comparing RPL Evidence:

** Ensuring Alignment with Industry Standards:*
Unit Standards and qualifications provided by Qualifications Authorities serve as benchmarks for competency and proficiency in various industries and fields. By comparing RPL evidence against these standards, institutions can ensure that learners meet the required skill levels expected by employers and industry stakeholders.

** Establishing Consistency and Reliability:*
The comparison process helps maintain consistency and reliability in RPL assessments. By aligning RPL evidence with established

standards, institutions can ensure that assessment decisions are fair, transparent, and consistent across different contexts and assessors.

Facilitating Credit Transfer and Articulation:

Comparing RPL evidence against Unit Standards and qualifications enables learners to receive credits or exemptions for further study or training. This process facilitates credit transfer and articulation pathways, allowing learners to progress seamlessly within the education and training system.

Validating the RPL Process:

Comparing RPL evidence against established standards provides validation for the RPL process itself. It demonstrates that RPL assessments are accurate, credible, and aligned with industry requirements, thereby enhancing the confidence of stakeholders, including learners, employers, and education providers.

The Role of Assessors and Qualifications Authorities:

** Expertise of Assessors:*

It is important that trained assessors compare RPL evidence against Unit Standards and qualifications. Their expertise ensures that assessments are conducted accurately and fairly, and considering the specific requirements of each qualification or Unit Standard.

** Co-operation with Qualifications Authorities:*

Co-operation between RPL providers and Qualifications Authorities is necessary to maintain the integrity of the comparison process. Qualifications Authorities provide guidance on the interpretation and application of Unit Standards and qualifications, ensuring alignment with industry expectations.

Challenges and Considerations:

** Complexity of Standards:*

Unit Standards and qualifications may vary in complexity and specificity, posing challenges for assessors in comparing RPL evidence. Clear guidelines and training programs can help address these challenges and ensure consistent and accurate *assessments*.

** Access to Information:*

Access to up-to-date information on Unit Standards and qualifications is crucial for RPL providers and assessors. Close co-operation with Qualifications Authorities and ongoing professional development can help ensure that assessors remain informed about relevant standards and requirements.

The necessity of comparing RPL evidence against Unit Standards, part qualifications, or full qualifications, provided by Qualifications Authorities cannot be overstated. This comparison process ensures alignment with industry standards, establishes consistency and reliability in assessments, facilitates credit transfer and articulation, and validates the RPL process itself. By embracing this practice, RPL providers can enhance the credibility and effectiveness of RPL assessments, ultimately empowering learners to achieve their educational and career goals.

Chapter 5

Roles and Responsibilities of Stakeholders

Now that we have a basic understanding of the RPL assessment process, we discuss the roles and responsibilities of the various stakeholders involved. In any RPL process, there are typically three main stakeholders:
* The learner,
* The assessor, and
* The institution.

Learner:

The learner benefits most from the RPL process, and gathering evidence, participating in assessments, and engaging in self-reflection, is important.

The learner's responsibilities may include:

- Expressing and communicating their prior learning experiences and aspiration
- Identifying and gathering evidence to support their claims of prior learning.
- Participating actively in the assessment process and providing additional information or clarification as needed.
- Reflecting on feedback and using it to inform their ongoing learning and development.

Assessor:

The assessor is responsible for evaluating the learner's evidence and making decisions regarding their eligibility for RPL. The assessor's responsibilities may include:

- Reviewing the evidence submitted by the learner and assessing its relevance, authenticity, and sufficiency.
- Applying established assessment criteria to determine whether the learner meets the requirements for RPL.
- Providing timely and constructive feedback to the learner throughout the assessment process.
- Ensuring that the assessment process is fair, transparent, and consistent.

Institution:

The institution, whether it is a university, college, training provider, or employer, plays a crucial role in facilitating the RPL process and ensuring its integrity and effectiveness. The institution's responsibilities may include:

- Providing information and guidance to learners about the RPL process and requirements.
- Designing and implementing RPL policies and procedures that align with industry standards and regulatory requirements.
- Training and supporting assessors to ensure they have the knowledge, skills, and resources needed to conduct assessments effectively.
- Ensuring that the RPL process complies with legal and ethical standards and respects the rights and privacy of learners.

Let's look at this in more detail:

Roles and Responsibilities of Stakeholders (Learner, Assessor, Institution)

In Recognition of Prior Learning (RPL), each stakeholder plays an important role, and contributes to the success and integrity of the assessment process. Whether you are a learner eager to demonstrate your skills, an assessor tasked with evaluating evidence, or an institution committed to facilitating RPL opportunities, understanding your role and responsibilities is important in ensuring a smooth and effective RPL process.

The roles and responsibilities of each stakeholder are as follows:

1. The Learner:

As a learner seeking recognition for your prior learning, you are the main character, driving the RPL process forward with your experiences, skills, and goals. But there are some important tasks the learner must complete:

** Self-Assessment:*

Start with introspection, reflecting on your experiences, skills, and knowledge to identify areas where you believe you already meet the requirements for formal recognition. This self-assessment lays the foundation for the evidence you'll gather and submit for assessment.

** Evidence Collection:*

Once you have identified the skills and knowledge you wish to have assessed, it is time to gather evidence to support your claims. This could include work samples, certificates, transcripts, references, or any other documentation that demonstrates your competence in the areas being assessed.

Submission and Participation:

Submit your evidence to the designated RPL assessor or assessment panel and actively participate in the assessment process. This may involve providing additional information or clarification as requested by the assessor(s) and engaging in assessment activities, like interviews, observations, or practical demonstrations.

** Feedback and Reflection:*

Following the assessment, you will receive feedback on your performance and the outcome of the assessment. Carefully look at the feedback, reflecting on your strengths and areas for improvement, and consider how you can continue to grow and develop in your educational and professional journey.

** Advocacy and Empowerment:*

Finally, as a learner engaged in the RPL process, you help yourself and assist others, promoting the value of RPL and its potential to empower individuals to achieve their educational and career goals. Share your RPL success stories and inspire others to start their own RPL journeys.

2. The Assessor:

The assessor empowers the RPL process, evaluating evidence and making informed decisions about the recognition of prior learning. As an assessor, you hold a position of trust and authority, and your role is very important in ensuring the fairness, validity, and reliability of the assessment process. Here's what the assessor's responsibilities involve:

** Competency and Impartiality:*

As an assessor, you must possess the necessary knowledge, skills, and expertise to assess the evidence provided by learners accurately. You must also maintain impartiality and objectivity throughout the assessment process, avoiding bias or favouritism in your judgments.

**Evidence Evaluation:*

Your primary responsibility is to evaluate the evidence submitted by learners against the established criteria or standards for the qualification or certification being sought. This may involve reviewing documentation, conducting interviews, or observing practical demonstrations to assess competency.

Clear Communication:

Throughout the assessment process, you must communicate clearly and effectively with learners, providing guidance on the evidence requirements, assessment procedures, and expectations. You should also ensure that learners understand their rights and responsibilities in the RPL process.

Feedback and Decision Making:

After evaluating the evidence, you will provide feedback to learners on their performance and the outcome of the assessment. This feedback should be constructive, highlighting strengths, areas for improvement, and recommendations for further learning or development. Based on your assessment, you will decide whether the learner meets the requirements for RPL and is eligible for formal recognition.

Professional Development:

As an assessor, it is essential to engage in ongoing professional development to stay up-to-date and informed of best practices, trends, and developments in RPL assessment. This may involve attending training workshops, participating in peer review processes, or pursuing relevant qualifications or certifications.

3. The Institution:

The institution arranges the RPL process, and is responsible for creating an environment that enables, supports, and facilitates RPL opportunities for learners. Whether you are a university, college, training provider, or employer, your role in the RPL process has many levels and is important to a successful RPL process.

Here is what you need to know:

** Policy Development:*

As an institution, you are responsible for developing and implementing RPL policies and procedures that align with national or industry standards and regulations. These policies should outline the eligibility criteria, evidence requirements, assessment procedures, and appeals processes for RPL assessment.

** Support and Guidance:*

You must provide learners with the support and guidance they need to navigate the RPL process successfully. This may include offering information sessions, workshops, or one-on-one advising sessions to help learners understand the RPL requirements and prepare their evidence for assessment.

** Assessment Coordination:*

You are also responsible for coordinating the RPL assessment process, including appointing qualified assessors, establishing assessment panels, and ensuring the integrity and fairness of the assessment procedures. This may involve managing assessment schedules, allocating resources, and monitoring assessment outcomes.

Quality Assurance:

As an institution, you have a duty to ensure the quality and integrity of the RPL process through ongoing monitoring, evaluation, and review. This may involve conducting internal audits, getting feedback from stakeholders, and implementing improvements to enhance the effectiveness and efficiency of RPL assessment.

Recognition and Accreditation:

Finally, you are responsible for formally recognizing and accrediting the prior learning of learners who successfully demonstrate their competence through the RPL assessment process. This may involve awarding credits towards a qualification, granting exemptions from certain courses or modules, or conferring a full qualification or certification based on RPL outcomes.

The roles and responsibilities of stakeholders in the RPL process are interconnected and interdependent, each contributing to the success and integrity of the assessment journey.

Chapter 6

The Case for Equivalence in
Final Summative Assessments for RPL

The principle of equity and fairness is extremely important in the field of education and credentialing. Recognition of Prior Learning (RPL) offers a pathway for individuals to have their skills and knowledge assessed and accredited, often based on experiences gained outside formal education settings. However, ensuring equality in the final summative assessments for RPL, compared to non-RPL students, is essential to uphold the credibility and integrity of the qualification process.

This chapter investigates the reasons behind the requirement for equivalence in final summative assessments, drawing insights from research and evidence from esteemed Qualifications Authorities.

Importance of Equivalence in Final Summative Assessments

The fact that final summative assessments for RPL should be the same as for non-RPL students is based on principles of fairness, transparency, and academic accuracy. It ensures that individuals who have undergone the RPL process are held to the same standards and expectations as their peers who have followed traditional educational pathways. This equivalence is crucial for maintaining the credibility and trustworthiness of qualifications conferred through RPL.

Research Insights and Evidence

Research conducted by prominent Qualifications Authorities around the world, supports the necessity of equivalence in final summative assessments for RPL. For example, the South African Qualifications Authority (SAQA) emphasizes the need for alignment between RPL assessments and standard assessment practices to maintain the integrity of qualifications. Similarly, the National Qualifications Authority of Ireland (QQI) advocates for accurate and consistent assessment standards for both RPL and non-RPL students to ensure comparability and reliability.

Lessons from The Scottish Qualifications Authority (SQA)

The Scottish Qualifications Authority (SQA) provides valuable insights into the implementation of equality in final summative assessments for RPL. SQA's approach emphasizes the importance of assessing learners' skills and knowledge against the same standards and criteria, regardless of their entry route. This approach enhances confidence in the qualifications awarded through RPL and promotes consistency in assessment practices across the education system.

Guidance from The Office of Qualifications and Examinations Regulation (OFQUAL)

OFQUAL, as the regulator of qualifications, assessments, and examinations in England, emphasizes the need for comparability and fairness in assessment processes, including those related to RPL. By ensuring that RPL assessments align with established assessment principles and standards, OFQUAL aims to safeguard the quality and value of qualifications achieved through RPL pathways.

Upholding Standards and Equity

The requirement for equivalence in final summative assessments for RPL is essential for upholding academic standards, ensuring equity, and maintaining public trust in qualifications. Drawing on insights from reputable Qualifications Authorities, it is evident that aligning RPL assessments with standard assessment practices is crucial for promoting consistency, comparability, and credibility in the education and training sector. Moving forward, institutions and policymakers must continue to prioritize and encourage equivalence in RPL assessments to support learners and uphold the integrity of qualifications.

The evidence presented from reputable Qualifications Authorities such as the South African Qualifications Authority (SAQA), the National Qualifications Authority of Ireland (QQI), the Scottish Qualifications Authority (SQA), and The Office of Qualifications and Examinations Regulation (Ofqual) collectively emphasizes the necessity for equality in final summative assessments between Recognition of Prior Learning (RPL) candidates and full course students.

Here is how the evidence supports the requirement for RPL candidates to undertake the same theoretical and practical assessments as full course students:

Alignment with Standard Assessment Practices:

SAQA emphasizes the need for alignment between RPL assessments and standard assessment practices. This means that RPL candidates should be subjected to the same assessment methods and criteria as full course students to maintain the integrity and credibility of qualifications.

Rigorous and Consistent Assessment Standards:

QQI endorses rigorous and consistent assessment standards for both RPL and non-RPL students. This suggests that RPL candidates must meet the same assessment standards as full course students to ensure comparability and reliability in the assessment process.

Assessing Against the Same Standards and Criteria:

SQA's approach highlights the importance of assessing learners against the same standards and criteria, irrespective of their entry route. Therefore, RPL candidates should be evaluated based on the same assessment criteria and standards as full course students to ensure fairness and equity in the assessment process.

Promoting Consistency and Comparability:

Ofqual stresses the need for comparability and fairness in assessment processes, including those related to RPL. By aligning RPL assessments with established assessment principles and standards,

Ofqual aims to promote consistency and comparability in the evaluation of RPL candidates.

Based on the evidence provided by these Qualifications Authorities, it is evident that for assessments to be fair and equitable, RPL candidates must undergo the same theoretical and practical assessments as full course students. This ensures that RPL candidates are held to the same standards and expectations as their peers, thus upholding the integrity and credibility of qualifications awarded through RPL pathways.

Chapter 7

Validity, Authenticity, Reliability, Currency, and Sufficiency

In assessment, VARCS stands for Validity, Authenticity, Reliability, Currency, and Sufficiency. This framework serves as a guiding principle for designing, implementing, and evaluating assessment practices in educational settings. Each component of VARCS plays a crucial role in ensuring the quality, fairness, and effectiveness of assessments.

We discuss each element in detail:

Validity:

Validity refers to the extent to which an assessment instrument accurately measures what it intends to measure. In other words, does the assessment assess the intended learning outcomes? Validity ensures that assessment tasks effectively capture the knowledge, skills, and competencies outlined in the curriculum or learning objectives.

Types of Validity:

There are various types of validity, including:

* Content validity (the degree to which assessment content represents the domain being assessed),

* Criterion-related validity (the connection between assessment scores and external criteria), and

* Construct validity (the extent to which assessment tasks measure the intended construct or trait).

Ensuring Validity:

To ensure validity, assessment designers must carefully align assessment tasks with learning objectives, curriculum standards, and instructional content. They can also conduct validity studies, pilot tests, and expert reviews to validate assessment instruments before their implementation.

**Authenticity:*

Authenticity refers to the degree to which assessment tasks mirror real-world contexts, tasks, and challenges relevant to learners' future roles or professions. Authentic assessments should reflect authentic activities and scenarios encountered in professional practice or everyday life.

**Characteristics of Authentic Assessments:*

Authentic (trustworthy) assessments are characterized by tasks that are meaningful, relevant, and engaging for learners.

They require critical thinking, problem-solving, and application of knowledge in authentic contexts.

**Designing Authentic Assessments:*

Designing authentic assessments involves creating tasks that simulate real-world challenges, such as case studies, projects, simulations, and performance-based assessments. Authentic assessments should provide opportunities for learners to demonstrate their skills and competencies in authentic contexts.

**Reliability:*

Reliability refers to the consistency, stability, and dependability of assessment results over time and across different contexts. Reliable assessments produce consistent outcomes when administered under similar conditions and are free from random error or variability.

Types of Reliability:

There are several types of reliability, including:

* Test-retest reliability (consistency of scores over repeated administrations),

* Inter-rater reliability (consistency of scores across different raters (tests) or assessors),

* Internal consistency reliability (consistency of scores across items within a single assessment).

Enhancing Reliability:

To enhance reliability, assessment designers can use standardized procedures, clear scoring rubrics (instructions and procedures), and training for assessors to ensure consistent administration and scoring of assessments. They can also conduct reliability analyses to assess the internal consistency and stability of assessment measures.

Currency:

Currency (up to date) refers to whether the assessment criteria and the evidence provided is up-to-date and the relevance of assessment content and tasks in relation to current knowledge, practices, and standards in the field or discipline. Assessments should reflect the most up-to-date information, theories, and practices relevant to the subject area.

Keeping Assessments Current:

To ensure currency, assessment developers should regularly review and update assessment content, resources, and references to reflect changes in the field or discipline. They can consult industry experts, professional organizations, and scholarly literature to stay informed about emerging trends and developments.

Relevance to Learners:

Currency in assessment is essential for maintaining learners' engagement, motivation, and relevance to their future aspirations and goals. Assessments should reflect current or modern issues, challenges, and opportunities relevant to learners' professional or academic pursuits.

Sufficiency:

Sufficiency refers to the suitability, capability, and completeness of assessment evidence needed to make valid and reliable judgments about learners' knowledge, skills, and competencies. Assessments should provide a comprehensive and representative sample of learners' performance across the intended learning outcomes.

Collecting Sufficient Evidence:

Assessment designers should ensure that assessment tasks cover a broad range of learning objectives and competencies, avoiding over-reliance on a single assessment method or task. They should provide clear guidelines and criteria for performance expectations to facilitate consistent and comprehensive assessment.

Balancing Depth and Breadth:

Sufficiency in assessment involves striking a balance between assessing depth of understanding and breadth of coverage across the curriculum. Assessments should offer opportunities for learners to demonstrate both depth of knowledge in specific areas and breadth of understanding across the broader domain.

In summary, V.A.R.C.S. framework involves Validity, Authenticity, Reliability, Currency, and Sufficiency as essential principles for designing and implementing high-quality assessments in education. By adhering to these principles, educators can ensure that assessments accurately measure learning outcomes, reflect real-world contexts, produce consistent results, remain current with industry standards, and provide sufficient evidence for making valid judgments about learners' achievements and competencies.

Chapter 8

Types of Evidence Accepted for RPL Assessment

In this chapter we discuss the various types of evidence accepted for RPL assessment.

In the search for RPL recognition, evidence is very important. Without evidence, the learner cannot prove the experience or skill to claim the qualification.

But not just any evidence will do, it must be credible, relevant, and persuasive enough to convince assessors of your competence in each subject or skill area.

So, what types of evidence are accepted for RPL assessment? Here are some common examples:

Types of evidence accepted for RPL:

1. Work Experience:
Work experience can also be defined as real-world experience. Work experience is one of the most valuable forms of evidence for RPL assessment, as it provides solid proof of your skills, knowledge, and expertise in a particular field or occupation. Whether you've spent years climbing the corporate ladder, running your own business, or honing your craft in workshops, your work experience speaks volumes about your abilities and achievements.

So, what kind of work experience counts as evidence for RPL assessment?

The short answer:

Any experience that is relevant to the qualification or certification you are seeking.

This could include full-time or part-time employment, freelance work, internships, apprenticeships, or even unpaid work placements. The key is to demonstrate how your work experience aligns with the learning outcomes or competencies required for the qualification, providing specific examples of tasks performed, projects completed, and challenges overcome.

For example, if you are seeking RPL for a project management qualification, you might submit evidence like project plans, reports, budgets, or stakeholder communications from your previous roles. Similarly, if you are applying for recognition in a technical field like engineering or IT, you could provide documentation of projects you have worked on, systems you have developed, or certifications you have obtained during your career.

2. Certificates and Qualifications:

Certificates and qualifications are the core of formal education and training. If you have completed any accredited courses, programs, or certifications relevant to the qualification you are seeking, these can serve as strong evidence of your competence and expertise in a particular subject or skill area.

Certificates and qualifications come in all shapes and sizes, from short courses and workshops to diplomas, degrees, and professional certifications. The key is to ensure that your credentials are from reputable institutions or training providers recognized within your industry or field of study. This may involve checking accreditation status, verifying course content and assessment methods, and confirming that your qualifications align with the learning outcomes or competencies required for the RPL assessment.

When submitting certificates and qualifications as evidence for RPL assessment, it is essential to provide clear documentation, including transcripts, course outlines, assessment results, and any other relevant supporting materials. This helps assessors evaluate the accuracy and relevance of your prior learning and ensures that you receive the appropriate recognition for your achievements.

3. Volunteer Work:

Giving back to your community can also be a form of learning. Volunteer work is another valuable source of evidence for RPL assessment, as it demonstrates your commitment, initiative, and willingness to contribute to the greater good. Whether you have volunteered with local charities, community organizations, or international NGOs, your volunteer experiences can provide valuable insights into your skills, values, and interests.

When selecting volunteer work as evidence for RPL assessment, focus on activities that are relevant to the qualification or certification you are seeking and highlight the skills and knowledge you have gained through your volunteer experiences. This could include leadership roles, project management responsibilities, teamwork skills, communication abilities, or specialized expertise in areas such as fundraising, event planning, or community outreach.

For example, if you are applying for RPL in a field like social work, counselling, or community development, you might submit evidence of your volunteer work with marginalized populations, support groups, or advocacy campaigns. Similarly, if you are seeking recognition in a leadership or management role, you could provide documentation of your volunteer experience organizing events, leading teams, or implementing strategic initiatives.

4. Personal Projects:

Personal projects are a unique form of evidence for RPL assessment, as they showcase your ability to apply your skills and knowledge in real-world contexts outside of formal education or employment. Whether you have pursued hobbies, passions, or entrepreneurial ventures, your personal projects can provide compelling evidence of your creativity, resourcefulness, and problem-solving abilities.

When selecting personal projects as evidence for RPL assessment, focus on projects that are relevant to the qualification or certification you're seeking, and highlight the skills you have developed and knowledge you have gained through your project work. This could include examples of creative work, like art, writing, or design projects, as well as practical projects, such as DIY renovations, gardening, or cooking.

For example, if you are seeking RPL in a creative field, like graphic design, photography, or writing, you might submit evidence of personal projects you have completed, such as portfolios, blogs, or published works. Similarly, if you are applying for recognition in a technical field like programming, engineering, or carpentry, you could provide documentation of personal projects you have undertaken, such as software development, building projects, or technical innovations.

Now that we have explored some common examples of evidence accepted for RPL assessment, let's look deeper into how to document this evidence effectively. After all, presenting your evidence in a clear, organized, and compelling manner is key to making a strong case for recognition of your prior learning.

In the next chapter, we discuss guidelines for documenting evidence effectively.

Chapter 9

Preparing for RPL Assessment

Introduction:

In this chapter we discuss:

*Preparing for Recognition of Prior Learning (RPL) assessment.

We will discuss everything you need to know to get yourself prepared and ready for the RPL assessment process.

Preparing for RPL assessment is a bit like preparing for a marathon. It requires careful planning, dedication, and a clear understanding of the challenges and opportunities that lie ahead. But with the right mindset and approach, you can navigate the RPL process and succeed with confidence.

So, what does it take to prepare for RPL assessment?

Let's break it down into three key components:

1. Self-assessment: Identifying prior learning and skills

Before you can start the RPL journey, you need to list your prior learning and skills. This includes what you know, what you've done, and what you are capable of. This process of self-assessment is a crucial first step in preparing for RPL assessment, as it lays the foundation for the evidence you will gather and submit to support your claims of competence.

Self-assessment involves reflecting on your educational, work, and life experiences, to identify the skills, knowledge, and competencies you've acquired along the way.

Ask yourself questions like:

* What experiences have shaped my understanding of this subject or skill?

* What tasks or projects have I completed that demonstrate my competence in this area?

* What feedback have I received from others about my performance in related activities?

By taking the time to reflect on your experiences and achievements, you can gain a clearer understanding of your strengths, weaknesses, and areas for development, which will inform your approach to gathering evidence for RPL assessment.

2. Gathering evidence and organizing documentation

Once you have identified your prior learning and skills, the next step is to gather evidence and organize documentation to support your claims of competence. This could include work samples, certificates, qualifications, references, personal projects, and any other documentation that demonstrates your skills and knowledge in the areas being assessed.

Gathering evidence for RPL assessment is a bit like collecting pieces of a puzzle. You want to gather a wide range of evidence sources that collectively paint a detailed picture of your competence and expertise. Be strategic in your selection of evidence, focusing on examples that best display your skills and achievements in relation to the RPL assessment criteria.

Once you have gathered your evidence, it is essential to organize it effectively to make it easy for assessors to review and evaluate. Use clear headings, subheadings, and labels to structure your evidence package logically, and provide context and background information to help assessors understand the significance of each piece of evidence.

3. Understanding the expected learning outcomes of the qualification.

In addition to self-assessment and evidence gathering, it is crucial to have a clear understanding of the expected learning outcomes of the qualification or certification you are seeking through RPL assessment. This involves familiarizing yourself with the curriculum, syllabus, or competency standards for the qualification, and identifying how your prior learning aligns with these expectations.

Understanding the expected learning outcomes will help you tailor your evidence package to meet the requirements of the RPL assessment and ensure that you are focusing on the most relevant and impactful examples of your prior learning. It will also allow you to prove how your skills and knowledge meet or exceed the standards set forth by the qualification, providing a compelling case for recognition.

In summary, preparing for RPL assessment is a complicated process that involves self-assessment, evidence gathering, and a clear understanding of the expected learning outcomes of the qualification. By taking the time to reflect on your experiences, gather relevant evidence, and align your skills with the assessment criteria, you can set yourself up for success in the RPL application.

Let's look at these in more detail:

1. Self-assessment: Identifying Prior Learning and Skills

Think of self-assessment as the compass that guides you through the maze of your prior learning and skills, helping you navigate the RPL assessment process with confidence and clarity.

Self-assessment is an important first step in preparing for RPL assessment, because it lays the groundwork for everything that follows. It is about taking a step back, reflecting on your experiences, and identifying the skills, knowledge, and competencies you have acquired along the way.

Here are some guidelines:

1. Reflect on Your Experiences:

The first step in self-assessment is to reflect on your experiences, both formal and informal, and consider how they have contributed to your learning and development. Think about your education, work, hobbies, volunteer activities, and life experiences, and ask yourself:

* What have I learned from these experiences?
    * What skills have I acquired or honed?
    * How have these experiences shaped my understanding of myself and the world around me?

Take the time to write down your thoughts and reflections, capturing key moments, insights, and achievements that stand out to you. This process of reflection will help you gain a deeper understanding of your strengths, weaknesses, interests, and areas for growth, which will inform your approach to gathering evidence for RPL assessment.

2. Identify Transferable Skills:

As you reflect on your experiences, pay special attention to the transferable skills you have developed; those versatile skills that can be applied across different contexts and settings. These could include skills like communication, problem-solving, teamwork, leadership, time management, and critical thinking.

Take a moment to brainstorm a list of transferable skills you possess, drawing from your experiences in education, work, and other areas of your life. Be specific and concrete in your descriptions, providing examples of how you have demonstrated each skill in different situations. This exercise will help you identify the strengths you bring to the table and highlight them in your evidence for RPL assessment.

3. Assess Your Knowledge and Competencies:

In addition to transferable skills, make a list of your knowledge and competencies in specific subject areas or fields of study. Consider the subjects you have studied, the certifications or qualifications you have obtained, and the practical skills you have developed through hands-on experience.

Make a list of the subjects or areas of expertise where you feel confident in your knowledge and competencies, noting any gaps or areas for improvement that you may need to address. This self-assessment will help you identify the areas where you may be suitable for RPL assessment and where you may need to focus your efforts on gathering additional evidence or upskilling.

4. Seek Feedback and Validation:

Once you have completed your self-assessment, consider seeking feedback and validation from others who know you well, colleagues, supervisors, mentors, friends, or family members. Share your reflections and insights with them, and ask for their input on your strengths, weaknesses, and areas for development.

Listen carefully to the feedback you receive. Keep an open mind and consider how it aligns with your own self-assessment. Use this feedback to validate your self-assessment findings, gain new perspectives on your skills and competencies, and identify any blind spots or areas you may have overlooked.

5. Set Goals and Action Plans:

When you have completed the insights from your self-assessment and feedback, it is time to set goals and action plans for your RPL journey. Identify the qualifications or certifications you're interested in pursuing through RPL assessment, and establish clear, achievable goals for what you hope to achieve.

Break down your goals into smaller, manageable tasks, and create action plans for how you will gather evidence, organize documentation, and prepare for RPL assessment. Set deadlines and progressive goals to keep yourself accountable and track your progress as you work towards your goals.

Chapter 10

Gathering Evidence and Organizing Documentation

In this chapter investigate the important task of gathering evidence and organizing documentation to support your RPL application.

How to organize documentation to support the RPL application:

1. Identify Relevant Evidence Sources:

The first step in gathering evidence for RPL assessment is to identify relevant evidence sources that demonstrate your skills, knowledge, and competencies in the areas being assessed.

This could include a wide range of materials, such as:

Work samples:

Reports, presentations, projects, or portfolios that showcase your skills and achievements in the workplace.

Certificates and qualifications:

Diplomas, degrees, certifications, or licenses that demonstrate your formal education and training.

References and testimonials:

Letters of recommendation, performance evaluations, or testimonials from supervisors, colleagues, or clients.

Personal projects:

Creative or practical projects that demonstrate your skills and expertise in a particular area.

Volunteer work:

Records, reports, or testimonials from volunteer activities that highlight your contributions and accomplishments.

Other documentation:

Any other relevant documentation, such as awards, publications, or transcripts.

Take the time to brainstorm and make a list of potential evidence sources based on your self-assessment and the expected learning outcomes of the qualification you're seeking through RPL assessment.

2. Collect and Compile Evidence:

Once you have identified relevant evidence sources, it is time to start collecting and compiling the evidence into an organized package that supports your RPL application. Be proactive and systematic in your approach, reaching out to employers, educational institutions, colleagues, and other relevant parties to gather the necessary documentation.

If you are collecting work samples, make sure to obtain permission from your employer or client to use the materials in your RPL application. Keep detailed records of the evidence you collect, including dates, sources, and any relevant contextual information that will help assessors understand the significance of the evidence.

As you collect evidence, organize it into categories or folders based on the assessment criteria or learning outcomes of the qualification you're seeking. This will make it easier to review and present the evidence to assessors and ensure that you're covering all the necessary bases.

3. Ensure Authenticity and Validity:

When gathering evidence for RPL assessment, it is crucial to ensure the authenticity and validity of the materials you are submitting. Avoid overdoing or falsifying evidence, as this could undermine the credibility of your application and lead to rejection or penalties.

Verify the authenticity of your evidence by cross-referencing it with other sources or obtaining corroborating evidence from reliable sources. For example, if you are submitting work samples, make sure they accurately reflect your contributions and achievements in the workplace, and consider providing supporting documentation or testimonials from supervisors or colleagues.

Similarly, if you are presenting certificates or qualifications as evidence, ensure that they are from accredited institutions or training providers recognized within your industry or field of study. Check the accreditation status of the issuing institution, verify the authenticity of the certificates, and provide any additional documentation or context that may be required to validate your qualifications.

4. Organize Evidence Effectively:

The way on which you present your evidence matters when it comes to organizing evidence for RPL assessment, so take the time to structure your evidence package in a clear, organized, and professional manner. Use clear headings, subheadings, and labels to categorize and organize your evidence, and provide context and background information to help assessors understand the significance of each piece of evidence.

Consider creating a digital portfolio or evidence file where you can store and organize your evidence in a centralized location. This could be a folder on your computer, a cloud-based storage platform, or an online portfolio website where you can showcase your work samples, qualifications, and other evidence to assessors.

Ensure that your evidence package is user-friendly, easy to navigate and review, with clear links or references between different pieces of evidence and a logical flow that guides assessors through your prior learning experiences and achievements. This will make it easier for assessors to assess your competence and expertise and make an informed decision about your eligibility for RPL.

5. Review and Refine Your Evidence:

Before submitting your evidence for RPL assessment, take the time to review and refine it to ensure that it is accurate, relevant, and compelling. Double-check the completeness and accuracy of your evidence package, making sure that you have included all the necessary documentation and addressed all the assessment criteria or learning outcomes of the qualification you're seeking.

Consider seeking feedback from trusted colleagues, mentors, or advisors who can provide constructive criticism and suggestions for improvement. Use their feedback to refine your evidence package, making any necessary revisions or updates to strengthen your case for RPL assessment.

Finally, proofread your evidence package carefully to detect any errors or inconsistencies in spelling, grammar, or formatting. Present your evidence in a professional and polished manner, paying attention to detail and ensuring that it reflects positively on your skills, knowledge, and professionalism.

Gathering evidence and organizing documentation for RPL assessment is a thorough and time-consuming process, but it is essential for demonstrating your prior learning and skills to assessors.

Identify relevant evidence sources, collect, and compile evidence systematically, ensuring authenticity and validity. Organize evidence effectively, and review and refine your evidence package.

Chapter 11

Understanding the Expected Learning Outcomes
of the Qualification

We must understand the critical task of understanding the expected learning outcomes of the qualification the learner is seeking through RPL assessment. By gaining a clear understanding of these outcomes, you will be better equipped to gather relevant evidence, organize documentation, and present a compelling case for recognition of your prior learning.

1. What are Learning Outcomes?

Before we investigate the specifics of expected learning outcomes, let's first clarify what we mean by this term. Learning outcomes are statements that describe the knowledge, skills, and competencies that learners are expected to demonstrate or achieve when completing a course, program, or qualification. These outcomes serve as benchmarks or standards against which learners' performance is assessed and measured.

Learning outcomes are typically written in clear, specific, and measurable terms, making it easy for assessors to evaluate whether learners have met the required standards of competence. They provide a roadmap or guide for both learners and assessors, outlining the key areas of focus and the desired outcomes of the learning process.

2. Why are Learning Outcomes Important?

Understanding the expected learning outcomes of the qualification you are seeking through RPL assessment is essential for several reasons:

Alignment:

Learning outcomes ensure that the content and assessment methods of a qualification are aligned with its intended purpose and objectives. They provide a clear framework for designing curriculum, developing learning materials, and assessing learners' performance, ensuring consistency and coherence in educational programs.

Transparency:

Learning outcomes make the expectations of a qualification clear and transparent to learners, helping them understand what is expected of them and what they need to achieve to succeed. This transparency promotes a sense of ownership and responsibility for their learning journey, empowering learners to take an active role in their education.

**Assessment:*

Learning outcomes serve as criteria for assessing learners' performance and progress throughout a qualification. They provide a basis for designing assessment tasks, evaluating learners' work, and providing feedback on their strengths and areas for improvement. By aligning assessment with learning outcomes, assessors can ensure that their judgments are fair, valid, and reliable.

**Recognition:*

Learning outcomes provide a basis for recognizing learners' prior learning and skills through RPL assessment. By comparing learners' existing knowledge and competencies against the expected learning outcomes of a qualification, assessors can determine whether learners are eligible for recognition and, if so, to what extent.

3. How to Identify Learning Outcomes:

To understand the expected learning outcomes of the qualification you are seeking through RPL assessment, start by reviewing the official documentation provided by the awarding body or institution responsible for the qualification.

This could include:

**Course outlines or syllabi:*

These documents typically provide an overview of the content, structure, and assessment methods of a qualification, as well as a list of learning outcomes or objectives for each unit or module. This will typically be in the form of Unit Standards or Qualifications with Assessment Criteria outlined by the Qualifications Authority.

**Competency standards or frameworks:*

If you are seeking recognition for a vocational qualification, you may need to refer to industry-specific competency standards or frameworks that outline the skills and competencies required for a particular occupation or role.

Qualification frameworks or descriptors:

National or international qualification frameworks often include descriptors or profiles that describe the expected learning outcomes of qualifications at different levels, helping learners and assessors understand the depth and breadth of learning required.

Review these documents carefully, paying close attention to the language used to describe the learning outcomes and the specific skills, knowledge, and competencies that are expected to be demonstrated. Look for keywords and phrases that indicate the desired outcomes of the qualification, such as "demonstrate," "apply," "analyse," "evaluate," or "synthesize."

4. Mapping Prior Learning to Learning Outcomes:

Once you have a clear understanding of the expected learning outcomes of the qualification, the next step is to map (compare) your prior learning and skills against these outcomes. This involves identifying the areas where your existing knowledge and competencies align with the learning outcomes and where there may be gaps or areas for further development.

Start by reviewing your self-assessment and the evidence you have gathered to identify the skills, knowledge, and competencies you possess that are relevant to the qualification's learning outcomes. Look for examples or instances where you have demonstrated these attributes in your prior learning experiences, such as work projects, educational achievements, or personal accomplishments.

As you compare your prior learning to the learning outcomes, consider the depth and breadth of your knowledge and competencies in each area.

Are there specific learning outcomes where you feel particularly strong, or where you may need additional evidence to support your claims?

Are there any gaps or areas where you may need to upskill, or acquire new knowledge to meet the required standards?

5. Developing a Learning Plan:

Based on your self-assessment and the alignment between your prior learning and the expected learning outcomes of the qualification, develop a learning plan that outlines your goals, objectives, and strategies for filling any gaps or addressing any areas for improvement.

This could involve:

* Identifying additional evidence or documentation needed to support your RPL application, such as work samples, certificates, or testimonials.

* Undertaking further study or training to acquire new knowledge or skills that align with the learning outcomes of the qualification.

* Engaging in professional development activities, such as workshops, seminars, or online courses, to enhance your expertise in specific areas.

* Seeking guidance or support from mentors, coaches, or subject matter experts who can provide advice and assistance in areas where you may need help.

By developing a learning plan tailored to your individual needs and circumstances, you can take proactive steps to address any gaps or areas for improvement identified through your self-assessment and alignment with the expected learning outcomes of the qualification. This will not only strengthen your RPL application but also enhance your overall professional development and career prospects.

Understanding the expected learning outcomes of the qualification you are seeking through RPL assessment is essential for success in the assessment process. Familiarize yourself with the learning outcomes, compare your prior learning to these outcomes, and develop a learning plan to address any gaps or areas for improvement.

Chapter 12

Submitting Evidence for RPL Assessment

76

Introduction:
  Navigating the Evidence Submission Process

In this chapter, we will guide you through the process of submitting evidence for Recognition of Prior Learning (RPL) assessment. As you have gathered your evidence and organized your documentation, you are now ready to take the next step towards professionally showcasing your prior learning.

Submitting evidence for RPL assessment is a critical stage in the journey towards recognition of your skills and competencies. It is your opportunity to present a comprehensive and convincing case to assessors, demonstrating how your prior learning aligns with the expected standards of the qualification you're seeking.

In this chapter, we will provide you with step-by-step instructions for submitting your evidence, along with tips for presenting it effectively. We will also discuss the importance of communication with assessors and support staff throughout the process, ensuring that you have the guidance and assistance you need to succeed.

So, let's explore the fine points of submitting evidence for RPL assessment. With the right approach and mindset, you will be well on your way to achieving recognition for your prior learning and advancing your educational and career goals.

Step-by-Step Instructions for Submitting Evidence

Congratulations on reaching the stage of submitting evidence for your Recognition of Prior Learning (RPL) assessment! This is an exciting milestone in your journey towards recognition of your skills and competencies. Now, let's break down the process into manageable steps to ensure that you submit your evidence effectively.

Step 1: Review RPL Guidelines

Before you begin, carefully review the RPL guidelines provided by your educational institution or RPL assessment provider. These guidelines will outline the specific requirements and procedures for submitting evidence, including deadlines, formats, and any additional documentation that may be required.

Step 2: Organize Your Evidence

Ensure that your evidence is well-organized and clearly labelled according to the assessment criteria or learning outcomes of the qualification you are seeking. Use clear headings, subheadings, and labels to categorize your evidence and make it easy for assessors to navigate and review.

Step 3: Double-Check Documentation

Before submitting your evidence, double-check that all documentation is complete, accurate, and up to date. Make sure that you have included all the necessary materials, like work samples, certificates, qualifications, and any other supporting documentation required.

Step 4: Follow Submission Instructions

Follow the submission instructions provided in the RPL guidelines carefully. This may involve submitting your evidence electronically through an online platform, mailing physical copies to the assessment provider, or delivering them in person to a designated location.

Step 5: Include a Cover Letter or Statement

Consider including a cover letter or statement with your evidence package, summarizing your prior learning experiences, highlighting key achievements, and explaining how your evidence aligns with the assessment criteria or learning outcomes of the qualification. This can provide context and insight for assessors as they review your evidence.

Step 6: Keep Copies for Your Records

Make copies of all your evidence and documentation for your records before submitting them. This will ensure that you have a backup in case of loss or damage and will allow you to refer to your evidence during the assessment process or for future reference.

Step 7: Submit Before the Deadline

Submit your evidence before the deadline specified in the RPL guidelines to ensure that it is reviewed in a timely manner. Late submissions may not be accepted, so be sure to plan and allow yourself enough time to gather and prepare your evidence effectively.

Step 8: Follow Up if Necessary.

If you have any questions or concerns about the submission process, don't hesitate to reach out to the assessors or support staff for assistance. They are there to help you navigate the process and ensure that your evidence is submitted successfully.

Submitting evidence for RPL assessment may seem intimidating, but by following these step-by-step instructions and guidelines, you can ensure that your evidence is presented effectively and accurately. Remember to stay organized, communicate with assessors and support staff as needed, and take pride in displaying your prior learning.

Tips for Presenting Evidence Effectively

Now, let's discuss how to present that evidence in a way that maximizes its impact and effectiveness. Here are some tips to help you prove your prior learning:

1. Be Selective:

When presenting evidence, quality matters more than quantity. Focus on selecting the most relevant and compelling examples that demonstrate your skills, knowledge, and competencies in relation to the assessment criteria or learning outcomes of the qualification you are seeking. Choose evidence that showcases your best work and aligns closely with the expectations of the assessment.

2. Provide Context:

Context is important to helping assessors understand the significance of your evidence. When presenting work samples or projects, provide background information about the context in which they were completed, including the goals, objectives, challenges, and outcomes of the work. Explain the relevance of each piece of evidence to the assessment criteria or learning outcomes, and highlight any specific skills or competencies demonstrated.

3. Use Multiple Formats:

Consider presenting your evidence in a variety of formats to cater to different learning styles and preferences. This could include written documents, visual materials such as charts or graphs, multimedia presentations, or interactive demonstrations. Choose formats that best showcase your evidence and make it easy for assessors to understand and evaluate.

4. Organize Effectively:

Organize your evidence in a logical and coherent manner to make it easy for assessors to navigate and review. Use clear headings, subheadings, and labels to categorize your evidence according to the assessment criteria or learning outcomes and provide brief explanations or summaries where necessary to guide assessors through your evidence package.

5. Use Clear and Concise Language:

When describing your evidence, use clear and concise language that communicates your ideas effectively. Avoid jargon or technical language that may be unfamiliar to assessors and focus on providing straightforward explanations and descriptions that are easy to understand. Be specific and concrete in your descriptions, providing examples and evidence to support your claims.

6. Highlight Achievements:

Do not be afraid to highlight your achievements and successes in your evidence presentation. Show projects, initiatives, or accomplishments where you made a significant impact or achieved outstanding results. Use measurable data or standards where possible to assess the impact of your work and demonstrate the value your experience and how it compares to the assessment criteria.

7. Include Reflections:

Incorporate reflections or insights into your evidence presentation to provide assessors with a deeper understanding of your learning and development. Share your thoughts, observations, and lessons learned from your experiences, and discuss how they have shaped your understanding and approach to your field or profession. Reflecting on your experiences demonstrates critical thinking skills and adds depth to your evidence.

8. Seek Feedback:

Before finalizing your evidence presentation, seek feedback from trusted colleagues, mentors, or advisors who can provide constructive criticism and suggestions for improvement. Consider their input carefully and make any necessary revisions or refinements to strengthen your presentation.

9. Practice Presenting:

Practice presenting your evidence to yourself or a small audience before the actual assessment. This will help you become more comfortable with organizing your ideas and presenting your evidence effectively.

10. Be Professional:

Finally, approach your evidence presentation with professionalism and confidence. Dress appropriately, maintain a positive attitude, and demonstrate respect and courtesy towards assessors and support staff. Present yourself as a competent and capable candidate who is serious about their learning and development.

Presenting evidence effectively is essential for success in RPL assessment. By following these tips and strategies, you can demonstrate your prior learning in the best possible way and increase your chances of achieving recognition for your skills and competencies. So, take the time to prepare and present your evidence thoughtfully, and remember to approach the assessment process with confidence and enthusiasm.

Communication with Assessors and Support Staff

Communication is important when it comes to navigating the Recognition of Prior Learning (RPL) assessment process. Whether you have questions about the evidence submission process, need clarification on assessment criteria, or require support along the way, effective communication with assessors and support staff can make all the difference in your RPL journey. In this section, we will explore the importance of communication and provide tips for engaging with assessors and support staff effectively.

1. Understand the Role of Assessors:

It is essential to understand the role of assessors in the RPL assessment process. Assessors are responsible for reviewing your evidence, evaluating your prior learning against the assessment criteria, or learning outcomes of the qualification, and making decisions about your eligibility for recognition. They play a crucial role in ensuring that the assessment process is fair, transparent, and consistent.

2. Clarify Expectations and Requirements:

As you prepare to submit your evidence for RPL assessment, do not hesitate to reach out to assessors or support staff if you have questions or concerns about the process. Clarify any expectations or requirements regarding evidence submission, such as formatting guidelines, documentation requirements, or deadlines. Having a clear understanding of what is expected of you will help ensure that your evidence is prepared and submitted correctly.

3. Seek Guidance and Assistance:

If you are unsure about how to gather or present evidence effectively, do not be afraid to seek guidance and assistance from assessors or support staff. They are there to help you navigate the assessment process and can provide valuable advice and resources to support you along the way. Whether you need assistance with identifying relevant evidence sources, organizing documentation, or understanding assessment criteria, do not hesitate to reach out for help.

4. Provide Context and Explanation:

When submitting your evidence, consider providing context and explanation to help assessors understand the significance of your prior learning experiences. Include a cover letter or statement with your evidence package, summarizing your background, highlighting key achievements, and explaining how your evidence aligns with the assessment criteria or learning outcomes of the qualification. This can provide valuable insight for assessors as they review your evidence.

5. Respond to Feedback Constructively:

After submitting your evidence, be prepared to receive feedback from assessors on your application. Take this feedback constructively and use it as an opportunity to improve your evidence or address any areas of concern. If assessors request additional information or clarification, respond quickly, and provide the requested details to ensure that your application is processed efficiently.

6. Keep Lines of Communication Open:

Throughout the assessment process, keep lines of communication open with assessors and support staff. If you have questions or concerns at any stage of the process, do not hesitate to reach out for assistance. Similarly, if you encounter any challenges or issues, communicate them right away so that they can be addressed in a timely manner. Effective communication is essential for ensuring a smooth and successful RPL assessment process.

7. Stay Professional and Courteous:

Finally, remember to communicate with assessors and support staff in a professional and courteous manner. Be respectful of their time and expertise and follow any guidelines or protocols for communication that may be in place. By maintaining a positive and collaborative attitude, you'll promote productive relationships with assessors and support staff and contribute to a positive assessment experience.

Effective communication with assessors and support staff is essential for success in the RPL assessment process. By clarifying expectations and requirements, seeking guidance and assistance as needed, providing context and explanation for your evidence, responding to feedback constructively, keeping lines of communication open, and maintaining a professional and polite manner, you can navigate the assessment process with confidence and achieve recognition for your prior learning and skills.

Chapter 13

Assessing Prior Learning Evidence

Introduction:

Navigating the Assessment Process
We discuss the crucial process of assessing prior learning evidence.

As you have carefully gathered and submitted your evidence for Recognition of Prior Learning (RPL) assessment, it is now time to understand how assessors evaluate your evidence to determine your eligibility for recognition. This chapter will provide you with insights into the evaluation criteria, techniques, and principles that guide the assessment of prior learning evidence.

Understanding Evaluation Criteria:

Assessors use specific evaluation criteria to assess your evidence against the standards set by the qualification you are seeking through RPL. These criteria typically align with the expected learning outcomes and competencies of the qualification and may include factors such as relevance, currency, depth of knowledge, and quality of evidence. By understanding these criteria, you can ensure that your evidence effectively demonstrates your skills and competencies in the areas being assessed.

Exploring Techniques for Assessment:

Assessors use various techniques to assess competency and proficiency based on the evidence you have submitted. These techniques may include portfolio assessment, performance observation, interviews, written assessments, and validation of prior learning experiences. Each technique provides assessors with valuable insights into your skills, knowledge, and competencies, allowing them to make informed judgments about your eligibility for recognition.

Ensuring Reliability and Validity:

Reliability and validity are important principles in assessment, ensuring that the assessment process is fair, consistent, and accurate. Assessors work to ensure reliability by using standardized assessment methods, establishing clear criteria for evaluation, and conducting assessments in a consistent and unbiased manner. They also uphold validity by ensuring that the assessment accurately measures the intended learning outcomes and provides a true reflection of your skills and competencies.

Assessing prior learning evidence is a demanding and systematic process that involves evaluating evidence against established criteria, employing techniques to assess competency and proficiency, and ensuring reliability and validity in assessment. By understanding the evaluation criteria, techniques, and principles that guide the assessment process, you can prepare yourself effectively for the assessment of your prior learning evidence and increase your chances of success in achieving recognition for your skills and competencies.

So, let's discuss the details of assessing prior learning evidence and equip you with the knowledge and tools needed to navigate this important stage of the RPL assessment process.

Evaluation Criteria for Assessing Evidence

Assessing prior learning evidence is a thorough and detailed process that involves evaluating various aspects of the evidence submitted by the learner. Assessors use specific evaluation criteria to ensure fairness, consistency, and accuracy in the assessment process. In this section, we investigate the key evaluation criteria commonly used in assessing prior learning evidence.

1. Relevance:

One of the primary criteria for assessing evidence is its relevance to the learning outcomes or competencies being assessed. Assessors examine whether the evidence provided by the learner directly addresses the knowledge, skills, and competencies outlined in the qualification's standards or curriculum. Relevance ensures that the evidence accurately reflects the learner's prior learning experiences and their alignment with the requirements of the qualification.

2. Currency:

Assessors consider the currency of the evidence to determine its validity and applicability to the current context. They assess whether the knowledge, skills, and competencies demonstrated in the evidence are up-to-date and relevant to the current industry standards or practices. Currency ensures that the evidence reflects the learner's current level of proficiency and capability in the areas being assessed.

3. Depth of Knowledge:

Assessors evaluate the depth of knowledge demonstrated in the evidence to assess the learner's understanding and mastery of the subject matter. They look for evidence of critical thinking, analysis, synthesis, and application of knowledge in real-world contexts. Depth of knowledge indicates the learner's ability to go beyond surface-level understanding and engage with complex concepts and ideas.

4. Quality of Evidence:

The quality of evidence refers to the reliability, authenticity, and credibility of the information presented by the learner. Assessors assess the quality of evidence based on factors such as accuracy, completeness, clarity, and coherence. They look for evidence that is well-documented, supported by relevant documentation or products, and free from errors, conflicts, or inconsistencies.

5. Authenticity:

Assessors verify the authenticity of the evidence to ensure that it genuinely represents the learner's own work and experiences. They look for evidence that is original, genuine, and produced by the learner in their own capacity. Assessors may use various techniques, such as cross-referencing with other sources or conducting interviews, to validate the authenticity of the evidence submitted.

6. Sufficiency:

Assessors assess the sufficiency of evidence to determine whether it provides an adequate and comprehensive representation of the learner's prior learning experiences. They consider the quantity and diversity of evidence submitted by the learner, ensuring that it covers all relevant aspects of the learning outcomes or competencies being assessed. Sufficiency ensures that assessors have enough information to make informed judgments about the learner's skills and competencies.

Evaluation criteria play a crucial role in assessing prior learning evidence, guiding assessors in their evaluation of the relevance, currency, depth of knowledge, quality, authenticity, and sufficiency of the evidence submitted by the learner. By understanding and aligning with these criteria, learners can effectively prepare and present their evidence for assessment, increasing their chances of success in achieving recognition for their prior learning experiences.

Techniques for Assessing Competency and Proficiency

Assessing prior learning evidence is an important component of the Recognition of Prior Learning (RPL) process. It involves evaluating the knowledge, skills, and competencies that learners have acquired through their previous experiences, such as work, volunteering, or informal learning.

Here are various techniques used by assessors to assess competency and proficiency in prior learning evidence.

1. Portfolio Assessment:

Portfolio assessment is a widely used technique in RPL assessments. Learners compile a portfolio containing evidence of their prior learning experiences, such as work samples, certificates, qualifications, and reflective statements. Assessors review the portfolio to assess the learner's knowledge, skills, and competencies against the learning outcomes of the qualification being assessed. Portfolios provide a comprehensive overview of the learner's prior learning journey and allow assessors to evaluate their proficiency in various areas.

2. Performance Observation:

Performance observation involves directly observing learners as they demonstrate their skills and competencies in real-world or simulated settings. Assessors may observe learners performing tasks, completing assignments, or participating in practical activities relevant to the qualification being assessed. Performance observation provides valuable insights into the learner's ability to apply their knowledge and skills in authentic contexts, allowing assessors to assess their competency accurately.

3. Interviews:

Interviews are a valuable technique for gathering additional information about learners' prior learning experiences. Assessors conduct structured or semi-structured interviews with learners to explore their background, experiences, achievements, and areas of expertise. Interviews provide an opportunity for learners to elaborate on their prior learning experiences, provide context to their evidence, and demonstrate their understanding of key concepts. Assessors can use interviews to assess learners' depth of knowledge, critical thinking skills, and ability to articulate their learning experiences effectively.

4. Written Assessments:

Written assessments involve administering tests, quizzes, or written assignments to assess learners' understanding of key concepts, theories, and principles relevant to the qualification being assessed. Assessors may use written assessments to evaluate learners' ability to analyse information, solve problems, and communicate ideas effectively. Written assessments provide a standardized and objective measure of learners' knowledge and competencies, allowing assessors to assess their proficiency in specific areas.

5. Practical Demonstrations:

Practical demonstrations involve learners showcasing their skills and competencies through hands-on activities or tasks. Assessors may ask learners to complete practical exercises, simulations, or role-plays that simulate real-world scenarios relevant to the qualification being assessed. Practical demonstrations allow assessors to observe learners' skills in action, assess their ability to apply theoretical knowledge in practical situations, and evaluate their performance against industry standards.

6. Peer Review:

Peer review involves other professionals or subject matter experts in the assessment process to provide feedback and validation of learners' evidence. Peers may review learners' evidence and provide insights, suggestions, or recommendations based on their expertise and experience. Peer review adds an additional layer of validation and ensures that assessments are fair, unbiased, and reflective of industry standards and best practices.

7. Simulation Exercises:

Simulation exercises involve creating simulated scenarios or environments that mimic real-world situations relevant to the qualification being assessed. Learners are tasked with navigating the simulated scenario, making decisions, and solving problems as they would in a real-world setting. Assessors observe learners' responses, decision-making processes, and problem-solving skills during the simulation exercise, allowing them to assess their competency and proficiency in action.

8. Case Studies and Projects:

Case studies and projects provide learners with an opportunity to apply their knowledge and skills to real-world problems or challenges. Learners may be tasked with analysing case studies, developing solutions, or completing project-based assignments that demonstrate their ability to apply theoretical concepts in practical settings. Assessors evaluate learners' performance and outcomes of the case study or project, assessing their competency and proficiency in solving complex problems and achieving desired outcomes.

Assessing competency and proficiency in prior learning evidence requires a diverse range of techniques, including portfolio assessment, performance observation, interviews, written assessments, practical demonstrations, peer review, simulation exercises, and case studies and projects.

When employing these techniques strategically, assessors can gain a comprehensive understanding of learners' skills, knowledge, and abilities and make informed judgments about their eligibility for recognition of prior learning.

Chapter 14

Ensuring Reliability and Validity in Assessment

97

When it comes to assessing prior learning evidence, ensuring reliability and validity is very important. Reliability refers to the consistency and stability of assessment results, while validity concerns the accuracy and relevance of the assessment in measuring what it intends to measure. In this chapter, we will explore strategies and best practices for ensuring reliability and validity in the assessment of prior learning evidence.

1. Standardization of Assessment Procedures:

One key strategy for ensuring reliability in assessment is the standardization of assessment procedures. This involves clearly defining assessment tasks, criteria, and procedures to ensure consistency across assessments. By standardizing assessment procedures, assessors can minimize variability in assessment outcomes and enhance the reliability of the assessment process.

2. Training and Calibration of Assessors:

Another important factor in ensuring reliability is the training and calibration of assessors. Assessors should receive full training on assessment procedures, criteria, and standards to ensure consistency in their judgments. Regular evaluation and review sessions, where assessors review and discuss assessment decisions, can help maintain consistency and reliability across assessments.

3. Use of Rubrics and Assessment Criteria:

Rubrics (rules and guidelines) and assessment criteria provide clear guidelines for assessing prior learning evidence and ensure consistency in assessment judgments. Rubrics outline specific criteria and performance levels for each assessment task, making it easier for assessors to evaluate evidence objectively and consistently. By using rubrics and assessment criteria, assessors can ensure that assessment decisions are based on established standards and principles.

A rubric is an assessment tool that clearly indicates achievement (outcome) criteria across all the components of the qualification.

4. Triangulation of Evidence:

Triangulation of evidence involves gathering multiple sources of evidence to verify assessment judgments and enhance the validity of the assessment process. Assessors should seek evidence from diverse sources, such as portfolios, interviews, observations, and written assessments, to gain a comprehensive understanding of learners' skills and competencies. Triangulation of evidence helps ensure that assessment decisions are based on an all-inclusive view of learners' abilities and experiences.

5. Peer Review and Moderation:

Peer review and moderation is about involving other assessors or subject matter experts in the assessment process to review and validate assessment decisions. Peer review provides an additional layer of inspection and analysis, and ensures that assessment decisions are fair, consistent, and reliable. Moderation sessions, where assessors discuss and review assessment decisions, can help identify and address any discrepancies or inconsistencies in assessment judgments.

6. Transparency and Accountability:

Transparency and accountability are essential for maintaining the reliability and validity of the assessment process. Assessors should be transparent about assessment criteria, procedures, and decisions, ensuring that learners understand how their evidence will be evaluated. Additionally, assessors should be accountable for their assessment decisions, providing rationale and justification for their judgments to ensure transparency and fairness.

7. Continuous Improvement and Evaluation:

Continuous improvement and evaluation are crucial for enhancing the reliability and validity of the assessment process over time. Assessors should regularly review and evaluate assessment procedures, criteria, and outcomes to identify areas for improvement and make necessary adjustments. By engaging in continuous improvement and evaluation, assessors can ensure that the assessment process remains thorough, accurate, fair, and effective.

Ensuring reliability and validity in the assessment of prior learning evidence requires careful planning, standardization of procedures, training and calibration of assessors, use of rubrics and assessment criteria, triangulation of evidence, peer review and moderation, transparency and accountability, and continuous improvement and evaluation. By implementing these strategies and best practices, assessors can enhance the reliability and validity of the assessment process, ultimately providing learners with fair and accurate assessments of their prior learning experiences.

Chapter 15

Unmasking the Necessity of Theoretical Assessment

In this chapter, we look deeper into the importance of theoretical assessment in the recognition of prior learning process.

Theoretical assessment plays a crucial role in evaluating learners' understanding of theoretical concepts and principles relevant to their chosen qualification.

Throughout this chapter, we will discover the necessity of theoretical assessment, and explore why it is essential for assessing learners' knowledge and understanding of key theoretical concepts. We will also provide valuable insights and tips for preparing for theoretical assessment, helping you chart your course to success.

Additionally, we will explore sample theoretical assessment questions. These questions are designed to challenge your understanding and critical thinking skills, providing you with an opportunity to demonstrate your theoretical knowledge in practice.

We discuss theoretical assessment and empower you to succeed in your recognition of prior learning journey.

We uncover the critical role of theoretical assessment and explore why theoretical assessment is not just a box to check, but an essential component of the recognition of prior learning process.

Understanding Theoretical Assessment:

Theoretical assessment involves evaluating learners' understanding of theoretical concepts, principles, and frameworks relevant to their chosen qualification. While practical skills are undoubtedly important, theoretical knowledge forms the foundation upon which practical expertise is built. Therefore, assessing theoretical understanding is crucial for ensuring that learners possess a solid understanding of the underlying principles and theories that guide their field of study.

Demonstrating Understanding:

Theoretical assessment allows learners to demonstrate their understanding of key concepts and principles in their chosen field. It provides them with an opportunity to showcase their ability to apply theoretical knowledge to real-world situations, analyse complex problems, and formulate informed decisions. By assessing theoretical understanding, assessors can determine the broadness of learners' knowledge and their readiness to progress in their studies or careers.

Ensuring Competency and Proficiency:
While practical skills are often the focus of RPL assessments, theoretical assessment is equally important for ensuring learners' competency and proficiency in their chosen field. A strong theoretical foundation is essential for success in practical applications, as it provides learners with the conceptual framework and critical thinking skills necessary to excel in their field. Therefore, assessing theoretical competency is important for ensuring that learners possess the required knowledge and skills to succeed in their chosen profession.

Meeting Industry Standards:
Theoretical assessment also plays a crucial role in meeting industry standards and accreditation requirements. Many professional bodies and accrediting agencies require learners to demonstrate proficiency in theoretical concepts and principles as part of their qualification process. By assessing theoretical understanding, RPL programs can ensure that learners meet these industry standards and are equipped with the knowledge and skills needed to succeed in their chosen profession.

Charting Your Course: Tips for Preparing

Now that we understand the importance of theoretical assessment, here are some tips for preparing effectively:

Review Key Concepts:
Take the time to review key theoretical components and principles relevant to your chosen qualification. Make sure you understand the underlying theories and frameworks that govern your field of study.

**Practice Application:*

Practice applying the knowledge of the theoretical components to real-world scenarios or case studies. This will help you develop a deeper understanding of how theoretical knowledge can be applied in practical situations.

**Seek Feedback:*

Do not hesitate to seek feedback from peers, mentors, or tutors. They can provide valuable insights and suggestions for improving your understanding of theoretical concepts and your ability to apply them effectively.

**Stay Organized:*

Organize your study materials and notes in a way that makes sense to you. Create study guides, flashcards, or summaries to help reinforce key concepts and principles.

Stay Updated:

Keep up to date of the latest developments and research in your field of study. Stay informed about emerging theories, trends, and best practices to ensure that your theoretical knowledge remains current and relevant.

Quest for Knowledge: Sample Theoretical Assessment Questions

To help you test your understanding of theoretical components, let's explore some sample theoretical assessment questions:

- Explain the theory of supply and demand and how it influences market prices.
- Discuss the principles of ethical decision-making in business and provide examples of ethical dilemmas.
- Describe the key components of Maslow's hierarchy of needs and how they influence human behaviour.
- Analyse the impact of globalization on international trade and economic development.
- Evaluate the role of leadership in organizational success and discuss different leadership styles.

These sample questions are designed to test your understanding of theoretical components and your ability to apply them in various contexts. Take your time to consider each question carefully and provide well-thought-out responses that demonstrate your knowledge and critical thinking skills.

Theoretical assessment is a critical component of the recognition of prior learning process. It allows learners to demonstrate their understanding of key theoretical concepts and principles, ensures competency and proficiency in their chosen field, meets industry standards, and prepares them for success in their studies or careers. By understanding the necessity of theoretical assessment and effectively preparing for it, learners can demonstrate their knowledge, skills, and readiness to progress in their chosen field.

Chapter 16

Charting Your Course: Tips for Preparing

Preparing for theoretical assessment is an important step in the recognition of prior learning (RPL) process. In this chapter, we explore practical tips and strategies to help you through the RPL process.

1. Understand the Assessment Criteria:

The first step in preparing for theoretical assessment is to understand the assessment criteria. Take the time to carefully review the assessment guidelines provided by your RPL provider or institution. Pay close attention to the specific theoretical concepts and principles that will be assessed, as well as the format and structure of the assessment.

2. Review Key Concepts and Theories:

Once you have a clear understanding of the assessment criteria, it is important to review key theoretical models, ideas, and theories relevant to your chosen qualification. Go back to your course materials, textbooks, and lecture notes, and revisit the foundational principles in your field of study. Make sure to focus on components that are likely to be assessed in the theoretical assessment.

3. Create a Study Plan:

Effective preparation requires a well-structured study plan. Break down your study sessions into manageable chunks and assign dedicated time to review key concepts, practice application, and complete practice questions. Be realistic about your study goals and set achievable milestones to keep yourself on track.

4. Use Study Aids:

Consider using a variety of study aids to reinforce your understanding of key concepts. Flashcards, summaries, mind maps, and concept maps can all be valuable tools for condensing complex information and facilitating active recall. Experiment with different study aids to find what works best for you and your learning style. (You may also find my other book on Memory enhancement very useful here. Title: *"Memory: Understand it to increase it"*. Visit our website at *ecoursez.com* for more detail.

5. Practice Application:

Theory is only valuable if you can apply it effectively in real-world scenarios. Look for opportunities to practice applying theoretical concepts to practical situations or case studies relevant to your field of study. This will not only help confirm your understanding of the material but will also prepare you for the types of questions you may get in the theoretical assessment.

6. Seek Feedback and Guidance:

Do not hesitate to reach out for feedback and guidance as you prepare for theoretical assessment. Connect with peers, mentors, or tutors, to discuss challenging concepts, exchange ideas, and seek clarification on any areas of confusion. Take advantage of any support services offered by your RPL provider, such as tutoring or academic advice.

7. Stay Organized and Manage Your Time:

Effective time management is also important to successful preparation. Create a study schedule that balances your other commitments and allows you to dedicate focused time to your studies. Break down your study sessions into smaller tasks, set specific goals for each session, and track your progress to ensure you stay on target.

8. Stay Positive and Stay Motivated:

Finally, maintain a positive attitude and stay motivated throughout your preparation. Accept that preparing for theoretical assessment is a gradual process that requires patience, perseverance, and determination. Mark your progress, stay focused on your goals, and remind yourself of the reasons why achieving your qualification is important to you.

Understanding the Importance of Preparation:

Before we investigate the specifics of preparation, let's take a moment to understand why it is so important.

Theoretical assessment forms a critical part of the RPL process, as it evaluates your understanding of key concepts and principles in your chosen field of study. By preparing thoroughly, you not only increase your chances of success in the assessment but also deepen your knowledge and confidence in your subject matter.

1. Familiarize Yourself with Assessment Criteria:

The first step in your preparation is to familiarize yourself with the assessment criteria. This involves carefully reviewing the guidelines provided by your RPL provider or institution. Pay close attention to the specific theoretical concepts and principles that will be assessed, as well as the format and structure of the assessment.

2. Review Key Concepts and Theories:

Once you have a clear understanding of the assessment criteria, it is time to review the key concepts and theories relevant to your qualification. Go back to your course materials, textbooks, and lecture notes, and revisit the foundational principles in your field of study. Make sure to focus on concepts that are likely to be assessed in the theoretical assessment.

3. Create a Structured Study Plan:

Effective preparation requires a well-structured study plan. Start by breaking down your study sessions into shorter, manageable sessions and allocate dedicated time to review key concepts, practice application, and complete practice questions. Be realistic about your study goals and set achievable milestones to keep yourself motivated.

4. Use a Variety of Study Aids:

Experiment with different study aids to reinforce your understanding of key concepts. Flashcards, summaries, mind maps, and concept maps can all be valuable tools for condensing complex information and facilitating active recall. Find what works best for you and integrate these aids into your study routine.

5. Practice Application:

Theory is only valuable if you can apply it effectively in real-world scenarios. Look for opportunities to practice applying the knowledge of theoretical components to practical situations or case studies relevant to your field of study. This will not only promote your understanding of the material, but also prepare you for the types of questions you may come across in the theoretical assessment.

6. Seek Feedback and Guidance:

Do not hesitate to reach out for feedback and guidance as you prepare for theoretical assessment. Engage with peers, mentors, or tutors to discuss challenging concepts, exchange ideas, and seek clarification on any areas of confusion. Take advantage of any support services offered by your RPL provider, such as tutoring or academic advice.

7. Stay Organized and Manage Your Time:

Effective time management is key to successful preparation. Create a study schedule that balances your other commitments and allows you to dedicate focused time to your studies. Break down your study sessions into smaller tasks, set specific goals for each session, and track your progress to ensure you stay on target.

8. Maintain a Positive Attitude:

Preparing for theoretical assessment is a gradual process that requires patience, perseverance, and determination. Mark your progress, stay focused on your goals, and remind yourself of the reasons why achieving your qualification is important to you.

Chapter 17

Quest for Knowledge:
Different Types of Theoretical Assessment Questions

In this chapter, we explore the different types of theoretical assessment questions you may get during the recognition of prior learning (RPL) process. Understanding the various question types is essential for effective preparation and successful performance in theoretical assessments.

1. Multiple Choice Questions (MCQs):

Multiple choice questions are a common type of theoretical assessment question. In an MCQ, you are presented with a question followed by a list of possible answers, typically labelled A, B, C, and D. Your task is to select the correct answer from the options provided. MCQs are designed to test your knowledge and understanding of specific concepts, theories, or principles.

Example:

Which of the following is an example of a renewable energy source?

A) Coal

B) Oil

C) Solar

D) Natural Gas

2. True/False Questions:

True or False questions present a statement, and you must determine whether the statement is true or false based on your understanding of the subject matter. These questions are often straightforward but require careful consideration to avoid common pitfalls such as double negatives or absolutes.

Example:

True or False: The Earth revolves around the Moon.

3. Short Answer Questions:

Short answer questions require you to provide a brief response to a specific question or prompt. These questions may ask you to define a concept, explain a process, or provide examples. Short answer questions typically require more than a simple yes or no response but are shorter than essay questions.

Example:

Define the term "Photosynthesis" and briefly explain the process.

4. Essay Questions:

Essay questions are more open-ended and require you to provide a detailed and structured response to a question or prompt. You are expected to demonstrate your knowledge, critical thinking skills, and ability to articulate ideas effectively. Essay questions may require you to analyse, evaluate, or discuss complex concepts or issues in depth.

Example:

Discuss the impact of climate change on biodiversity, providing examples and evidence to support your arguments.

5. Problem-Solving Questions:

Problem-solving questions present you with a scenario or problem and require you to apply your knowledge and skills to analyse the situation and develop a solution. These questions often involve mathematical calculations, data interpretation, or practical application of theoretical concepts.

Example:

A company produces 500 units of a product at a cost of $10 each. If the selling price of the product is $15, calculate the company's total profit.

6. Case Study Questions:

Case study questions involve the analysis of real-world scenarios or case studies related to your field of study. You are required to read and interpret the case study, identify key issues or problems, and propose solutions or recommendations based on your understanding of theoretical concepts and principles.

Example:

Read the case study provided and analyse the factors contributing to the company's declining market share. Propose strategies to improve the company's competitive position.

7. Matching Questions:

Matching questions require you to pair related items from two lists. You are presented with two columns, each containing a list of terms or phrases, and you must match the items from one column to the corresponding items in the other column. Matching questions assess your ability to recognize associations between concepts or terms.

Example:

Match each term in Column A with its corresponding definition in Column B.

Column A:

Supply

Demand

Price elasticity

Column B:

a. The quantity of a good or service that consumers are willing and able to purchase at a given price.

b. The responsiveness of quantity demanded to change in price.

c. The quantity of a good or service that producers are willing and able to offer for sale at a given price.

Chapter 18

Practical Outcome Assessment

In this chapter, we will explain the importance of practical assessment, and how it aligns with expected learning outcomes. We look at various examples of practical assessment tasks and criteria.

Understanding the Importance of Practical Assessment in RPL:

Practical assessment plays a vital role in the RPL process, as it allows candidates to demonstrate their ability to apply theoretical knowledge and skills in real-world contexts. Unlike theoretical assessment, which evaluates understanding of concepts, practical assessment focuses on the application and execution of knowledge in practical scenarios. It provides a holistic (all-inclusive) measure of competency and proficiency, reflecting the individual's readiness to perform tasks in a professional setting.

Aligning Practical Assessment with Expected Learning Outcomes:

Effective practical assessment must align closely with the expected learning outcomes of the qualification being assessed. This ensures that candidates are evaluated based on their ability to meet the specific requirements and standards set by the qualification framework. By aligning practical assessment tasks with expected learning outcomes, RPL providers can ensure the validity and reliability of the assessment process while providing candidates with clear standards for success.

Examples of Practical Assessment Tasks and Criteria:

Throughout this chapter, we will explain a variety of practical assessment tasks and criteria commonly used in RPL assessments. From simulated workplace scenarios to hands-on demonstrations and performance evaluations, these tasks are designed to evaluate candidates' ability to apply theoretical knowledge and skills in practical contexts. By examining real-world examples and criteria for practical assessment, you will gain valuable insights into what to expect and how to prepare for practical assessment in your RPL journey.

Let's look at the details of practical outcome assessment, so that we can understand its importance, align it with expected learning outcomes, and explore practical assessment tasks and criteria that pave the way for success in the recognition of prior learning process.

Importance of Practical Assessment in RPL

In education and professional development, the recognition of prior learning (RPL), is an opportunity for individuals to validate their skills and knowledge acquired through practical experiences. Practical assessment within the RPL framework is highly important, serving as an essential component in evaluating candidates' readiness for real-world application of their learning.

1. Authentic Evaluation of Skills:

Practical assessment provides an authentic (accurate) means of evaluating candidates' skills and competencies in real-world scenarios. Unlike theoretical assessments, which primarily test knowledge acquisition, practical assessments test the application and execution of skills within relevant contexts. This authenticity ensures that candidates are assessed on their ability to perform tasks and duties required in their field of study or profession.

2. Bridging Theory and Practice:

While theoretical understanding is important, it is the ability to demonstrate this knowledge in practical action that truly defines competence. Practical assessment bridges the gap between theory and practice, allowing candidates to demonstrate their ability to apply theoretical concepts in practical settings. This alignment ensures that candidates possess the necessary skills and capabilities to succeed in their chosen profession.

3. Validation of Experiential Learning:

Many individuals obtain valuable knowledge and skills through hands-on experiences gained in various professional, personal, or voluntary roles. Practical assessment provides a mechanism to validate this experiential learning and recognize its contribution to an individual's overall competency. By acknowledging and assessing prior practical experiences, RPL promotes inclusivity and diversity in educational pathways.

4. Enhancement of Employability:

Employers increasingly value practical skills and experience when making hiring decisions. Practical assessment in RPL equips candidates with tangible evidence of their abilities, enhancing their employability and marketability in the workforce. Employers can trust that RPL graduates have undergone rigorous assessment and possess the practical skills necessary to excel in their roles from day one.

5. Promotion of Lifelong Learning:

Practical assessment encourages a culture of lifelong learning by recognizing and rewarding individuals' ongoing efforts to develop and refine their skills. By providing pathways for individuals to showcase their practical abilities, RPL motivates lifelong learners to continue seeking new experiences, acquiring new skills, and adapting to evolving industry demands.

Practical assessment is very important in the RPL structure, and serves as a strong and valid mechanism for evaluating candidates' practical skills and competencies. By aligning practical assessment with expected learning outcomes, and providing examples of relevant tasks and criteria, RPL providers can ensure the validity, reliability, and fairness of the assessment process, and empower individuals to demonstrate their readiness for success in their chosen fields.

Understanding the Importance of Practical Assessment in RPL:

Practical assessment is the foundation of RPL, offering a hands-on evaluation of the candidates' ability to apply theoretical knowledge and skills in real-world scenarios. While theoretical assessment assesses understanding, practical assessment goes a step further by examining candidates' capacity to execute tasks, solve problems, and demonstrate competency in practical settings. This aspect is particularly important in professions where practical skills are vital, such as healthcare, trades, and vocational fields.

** Real-world Relevance:*

One of the key benefits of practical assessment is its direct alignment with real-world scenarios and job requirements. By evaluating candidates' performance in tasks mirroring those they'll encounter in their profession, practical assessment provides a realistic measurement of their readiness to enter the workforce. This ensures that RPL candidates possess the practical skills and abilities necessary for success in their chosen field, enhancing employability and promoting workforce readiness.

** Holistic Evaluation:*

Practical assessment offers an all-inclusive evaluation of candidates' competencies, including not only technical skills but also problem-solving abilities, critical thinking, communication, and teamwork. Unlike theoretical assessment, which may focus solely on knowledge acquisition, practical assessment considers how well candidates can apply that knowledge in diverse contexts and adapt to dynamic situations. This comprehensive evaluation provides a more accurate reflection of candidates' overall capabilities, enabling RPL providers to make informed decisions about their readiness for qualification recognition.

** Validation of Learning:*

Practical assessment serves as a powerful validation of candidates' learning experiences and achievements. For individuals who have gained skills and knowledge through non-traditional pathways such as work experience, volunteer work, or self-directed learning, practical assessment offers a means to demonstrate their proficiency and expertise in a tangible way. By recognizing and assessing prior learning in practical contexts, RPL acknowledges the value of diverse learning experiences and validates candidates' skills and competencies acquired outside formal education settings.

** Promoting Quality Assurance:*

Furthermore, practical assessment plays a crucial role in ensuring quality assurance and maintaining the integrity of RPL processes. By establishing clear assessment criteria, standards, and benchmarks aligned with industry expectations and qualification requirements, RPL providers can uphold the consistency and credibility of practical assessments. This promotes confidence among stakeholders, including employers, educators, and candidates, in the reliability and validity of RPL outcomes.

The importance of practical assessment in RPL cannot be overstated. It is important in evaluating a candidate's readiness for qualification recognition, providing a strong and healthy mechanism for assessing practical skills, validating learning experiences, and promoting quality assurance in RPL processes.

Why is this alignment crucial and how does it ensure the effectiveness and validity of the assessment process.?

Understanding the Significance of Alignment:

Aligning practical assessment with expected learning outcomes is fundamental to the RPL process. Expected learning outcomes outline the knowledge, skills, and competencies that candidates are expected to demonstrate upon completion of a qualification. By aligning practical assessment tasks with these outcomes, RPL providers ensure that candidates are assessed based on the specific criteria deemed essential for successful qualification attainment.

Enhancing Relevance and Authenticity:

When practical assessment tasks align with expected learning outcomes, they become more relevant and authentic to candidates' learning experiences and future professional roles. Tasks reflect the real-world demands and challenges that candidates will encounter in their field, ensuring that assessment criteria mirror the skills and competencies required for success in their chosen profession. This alignment enhances the authenticity of the assessment process, promoting a deeper connection between assessment activities and candidates' practical contexts.

Promoting Clarity and Transparency:

Alignment between practical assessment and expected learning outcomes promotes clarity and transparency for both candidates and assessors. Candidates must understand precisely what is expected of them and how their performance will be evaluated. Facilitate focused preparation and reduce uncertainty. Similarly, assessors have clear guidelines for evaluating candidates' performance against predetermined criteria, ensuring consistency and fairness in assessment decisions.

Validating Competency and Proficiency:

When practical assessment aligns with expected learning outcomes, it validates candidates' competency and proficiency in the specific skills and competencies outlined in the qualification framework. Candidates' ability to successfully complete practical tasks demonstrate their readiness to perform the duties and responsibilities associated with the qualification, reinforcing the credibility and reliability of the RPL process.

Ensuring Quality Assurance:

Alignment between practical assessment and expected learning outcomes is necessary for maintaining quality assurance in RPL processes. By adhering to established standards, and criteria, RPL providers ensure that assessments are rigorous, relevant, and aligned with industry expectations. This commitment to quality assurance enhances the credibility and trustworthiness of RPL outcomes, promoting confidence among stakeholders, including employers, educators, and candidates.

Facilitating Continuous Improvement:

Alignment between practical assessment and expected learning outcomes facilitates continuous improvement in RPL practices. By regularly reviewing and refining assessment tasks and criteria to ensure alignment with evolving industry standards and educational best practices, RPL providers can enhance the effectiveness and validity of the assessment process over time. This ongoing commitment to improvement ensures that RPL remains responsive to the needs of candidates and stakeholders and continues to deliver high-quality outcomes.

In principle, aligning practical assessment with expected learning outcomes is essential for ensuring the relevance, validity, and credibility of the RPL process. By aligning assessment tasks and criteria with the knowledge, skills, and competencies outlined in qualification frameworks, RPL providers validate candidates' readiness for qualification recognition and promote confidence in RPL outcomes.

Real-world scenarios and criteria used to evaluate candidates' practical skills and competencies.

1. Simulated Workplace Scenarios:

Simulated workplace scenarios are a common method used to assess candidates' ability to apply theoretical knowledge and skills in realistic workplace settings. For example, in a healthcare RPL assessment, candidates may be presented with a simulated patient case study and asked to demonstrate their clinical skills, decision-making abilities, and communication with patients and colleagues. Assessors evaluate candidates' performance based on predetermined criteria such as accuracy, efficiency, and professionalism.

2. Practical Demonstrations:

Practical demonstrations require candidates to perform specific tasks or procedures relevant to their field of study or profession. For instance, in a trades RPL assessment, candidates may be required to demonstrate their ability to use tools and equipment safely, follow technical procedures, and troubleshoot common issues. Assessors observe candidates' performance, assessing their technique, accuracy, and adherence to industry standards.

3. Portfolio Assessment:

A portfolio assessment involves candidates compiling evidence of their practical skills and achievements, such as work samples, project reports, and certificates. In an RPL assessment for project management, candidates may submit a portfolio showcasing their successful completion of projects, including project plans, budgets, and outcomes. Assessors review the portfolio to assess candidates' competency in project management principles and practices.

4. Role-playing Exercises:

Role-playing exercises provide candidates with an opportunity to demonstrate their interpersonal skills, problem-solving abilities, and decision-making under pressure. For example, in a customer service RPL assessment, candidates may participate in role-playing scenarios where they interact with simulated customers to resolve complaints or inquiries. Assessors evaluate candidates' communication skills, conflict resolution abilities, and customer satisfaction.

5. Practical Assignments:

Practical assignments involve candidates completing tasks or projects relevant to their field of study or profession. For instance, in an RPL assessment for graphic design, candidates may be tasked with creating a logo design for a fictitious company or designing a marketing campaign for a specific target audience. Assessors evaluate candidates' creativity, technical skills, and ability to meet client briefs.

6. Workplace Observation:

Workplace observation involves assessors observing candidates performing their job duties in their actual workplace environment. This method allows assessors to assess candidates' practical skills, professional conduct, and ability to apply theoretical knowledge in real-time. For example, in a nursing RPL assessment, assessors may shadow candidates during their shifts, observing their patient care practices, medication administration, and documentation skills.

Criteria for Assessment:

Regardless of the practical assessment method used, assessors rely on predetermined criteria to evaluate candidates' performance. Common criteria include accuracy, completeness, adherence to standards, problem-solving abilities, communication skills, and professionalism. These criteria provide a standardized framework for assessment, ensuring consistency and fairness in evaluation across candidates.

Practical assessment tasks and criteria play a vital role in evaluating candidates' practical skills and competencies in RPL assessments. By using a variety of assessment methods and criteria aligned with expected learning outcomes, RPL providers can accurately assess candidates' readiness for qualification recognition.

Chapter 19

Understanding the Expected Learning Outcomes of the Qualification

In this chapter, we discuss importance of understanding the expected learning outcomes of a qualification within the context of recognition of prior learning (RPL). Let's see why this understanding is pivotal and how it impacts various aspects of the RPL process.

Understanding the Blueprint:

Imagine going on a road trip without a map or destination in mind. Similarly, embarking on an RPL journey without understanding the expected learning outcomes of the qualification is akin to navigating aimlessly. Expected learning outcomes serve as the blueprint for qualification attainment, outlining the knowledge, skills, and competencies candidates are expected to demonstrate upon completion. Understanding these outcomes provides clarity and direction, guiding candidates, and assessors throughout the RPL process.

Informing Evidence Collection:

An understanding of expected learning outcomes informs the evidence collection process in RPL assessments. By aligning evidence with specific learning outcomes, candidates can strategically gather and present evidence that showcases their proficiency in the required areas. For example, if a learning outcome relates to project management skills, candidates may submit evidence of previous project plans, budgets, and outcomes to demonstrate their competency in this area.

Guiding Assessment Practices:

Expected learning outcomes also guide assessment practices in RPL. Assessors use these outcomes as a benchmark to evaluate candidates' evidence and performance against predetermined criteria. For example, if a learning outcome relates to communication skills, assessors may assess candidates' written and verbal communication abilities based on established criteria such as clarity, coherence, and effectiveness.

Supporting Quality Assurance:

Understanding expected learning outcomes supports quality assurance in RPL assessments. By ensuring that assessments align with expected outcomes, RPL providers uphold the integrity and validity of the assessment process. Consistency in assessment practices ensures that all candidates are evaluated fairly and objectively, regardless of their background or prior experience.

Facilitating Feedback and Improvement:

An understanding of expected learning outcomes facilitates meaningful feedback and opportunities for improvement in RPL. Assessors can provide targeted feedback to candidates based on their performance against specific learning outcomes, highlighting areas of strength and areas for development. This feedback informs candidates' learning journeys, empowering them to address gaps in their knowledge and skills effectively.

Enhancing Stakeholder Confidence:

Lastly, understanding expected learning outcomes enhances stakeholder confidence in RPL outcomes. Employers, educators, and other stakeholders can trust that candidates who have successfully demonstrated proficiency in the expected learning outcomes possess the necessary knowledge and skills to perform effectively in their chosen field. This confidence strengthens the credibility and recognition of RPL qualifications within the broader education and employment landscape.

Basically, understanding the expected learning outcomes of a qualification is necessary for the success of the RPL process. It provides direction, informs evidence collection and assessment practices, supports quality assurance, facilitates feedback and improvement, and enhances stakeholder confidence.

Chapter 20

Appeals and Feedback Process

131

In this chapter we explain the appeals and feedback processes within recognition of prior learning (RPL).
* Procedures for appealing assessment decisions,
* Strategies for delivering constructive feedback to learners, and the
* Importance of continuous improvement in the RPL process.

We investigate the details of each aspect, to understand their significance in upholding the integrity of the RPL journey.

Procedures for Appealing Assessment Decisions:

The procedures for appealing assessment decisions are crucial to ensuring transparency and fairness in the RPL process. When candidates disagree with assessment outcomes, they must have access to a formal appeals process. This process typically involves submitting a written appeal outlining the grounds for disagreement and providing supporting evidence. The appeal is then reviewed by an independent panel or judge, who assesses the validity of the appeal and decides based on established criteria. Transparency, impartiality, and timeliness are key principles that underpin the appeals process, ensuring that candidates receive a fair and equitable review of their concerns.

** Providing Constructive Feedback to Learners:*

Constructive feedback is a basis of effective RPL practices, empowering learners to understand their strengths and areas for improvement. When providing feedback, assessors should focus on specific examples, offering praise for demonstrated competencies and providing actionable suggestions for areas requiring development.

Feedback should be clear, constructive, and tailored to the individual learner's needs, promoting a culture of continuous learning and improvement. Additionally, feedback should be provided in a timely manner to maximize its impact and support learners' progress on their recognition journey.

** Continuous Improvement in the RPL Process:*

Continuous improvement is essential for enhancing the quality and effectiveness of the RPL process. RPL providers should regularly evaluate their assessment practices, feedback mechanisms, and appeals procedures to identify areas for enhancement. This may involve soliciting feedback from candidates, assessors, and other stakeholders, conducting internal audits or reviews, and benchmarking against industry standards and best practices. By embracing a culture of continuous improvement, RPL providers can adapt to evolving needs, enhance stakeholder satisfaction, and promote excellence in RPL practices.

This chapter highlights the critical importance of appeals and feedback processes in the RPL journey. By establishing transparent and robust procedures for appealing assessment decisions, delivering constructive feedback to learners, and embracing continuous improvement, RPL providers can uphold the integrity of the assessment process, support learners on their recognition journey, and promote excellence in RPL practices. As we navigate through this chapter, we gain a deeper understanding of how these processes contribute to the overall success and credibility of the RPL experience.

Appeals and Feedback Process

Effective feedback is not just about pointing out mistakes; it's about guiding learners toward improvement, empowering them to succeed in their recognition journey. Let's explore how RPL providers can deliver feedback that is insightful, actionable, and supportive.

Understanding the Purpose of Feedback:

Before looking into the specifics of providing constructive feedback, it's essential to understand its purpose.

Feedback in RPL serves multiple functions:

* It informs learners of their progress,
* Identifies areas for improvement,
* Reinforces strengths,
* Encourages reflection and growth.

By providing constructive feedback, RPL providers contribute to learners' development and success.

Key Principles of Constructive Feedback:

Constructive feedback is built on a foundation of key principles that ensure its effectiveness. Firstly, feedback should be specific and objective, focusing on observable behaviours and outcomes rather than personal characteristics. It should also be timely, provided shortly after assessment to maximize its impact. Additionally, feedback should be actionable, offering clear guidance on how learners can improve their performance.

** Tailoring Feedback to Individual Learners:*
Each learner is unique, with their own strengths, weaknesses, and learning styles. Therefore, feedback should be tailored to individual learners, considering their background, goals, and preferences. For example, some learners may prefer detailed written feedback, while others may benefit more from face-to-face discussions or multimedia presentations.

** Balancing Positive and Constructive Feedback:*
Effective feedback strikes a balance between positive reinforcement and constructive criticism. While it's important to acknowledge and celebrate learners' achievements and strengths, feedback should also address areas where improvement is needed. By providing a balanced mix of positive and constructive feedback, RPL providers motivate learners while guiding them toward growth and development.

** Encouraging Self-Reflection and Goal Setting:*
Constructive feedback should encourage learners to engage in self-reflection and goal setting. After receiving feedback, learners should be prompted to reflect on their performance, identify areas for improvement, and set specific, achievable goals for future development. This process empowers learners to take ownership of their learning journey and actively work towards improvement.

** Building a Supportive Learning Environment:*
Feedback should be delivered within a supportive learning environment that values open communication, mutual respect, and trust. Learners should feel comfortable seeking clarification, asking questions, and expressing concerns about their assessment results. RPL

providers play a crucial role in fostering this environment, encouraging collaboration and feedback exchange among learners and assessors.

Using Feedback for Continuous Improvement:

Lastly, feedback should be used as a spark for continuous improvement in the RPL process. RPL providers should collect and analyse feedback from learners, assessors, and other stakeholders to identify areas for enhancement. By incorporating feedback into the ongoing review and refinement of assessment practices, RPL providers can ensure the quality, relevance, and effectiveness of their services.

This means that providing constructive feedback to learners is an important part of the RPL process, empowering learners to succeed and grow.

RPL providers can enhance the learning experience and promote excellence in RPL practices, by:

* Adhering to key principles,
* Tailoring feedback to individual learners,
* Balancing positive and constructive feedback,
* Encouraging self-reflection and goal setting,
* Fostering a supportive learning environment,
* Using feedback for continuous improvement.

Chapter 21

The Evolution of RPL

Continuous improvement is the driving force behind excellence in recognition of prior learning (RPL). We explore the importance of ongoing refinement and enhancement in the RPL process, aiming to ensure its effectiveness, fairness, and relevance to learners, assessors, and stakeholders alike.

Recognition of prior learning is not static; it evolves alongside advancements in education, technology, and industry practices. Continuous improvement acknowledges this evolution, recognizing the need to adapt and innovate to meet the changing needs of learners and industries. By embracing continuous improvement, RPL providers can stay ahead of the curve and deliver high-quality, future-ready assessment services.

Feedback as a seed for Improvement:

Feedback from learners, assessors, and stakeholders serves as a valuable source of insights for continuous improvement in the RPL process. By soliciting and analysing feedback, RPL providers can identify strengths, weaknesses, and areas for enhancement in assessment practices, policies, and procedures. This feedback-driven approach ensures that RPL remains responsive to the needs and expectations of its stakeholders.

Regular Review and Evaluation:

Continuous improvement involves regular review and evaluation of RPL practices to assess their effectiveness and impact. RPL providers should establish mechanisms for collecting, analysing, and acting upon data related to assessment outcomes, learner satisfaction, and stakeholder feedback. Through systematic evaluation, RPL providers can identify areas of success and areas in need of improvement, driving targeted interventions and enhancements.

** Staying Up to Date with Best Practices:*

In the rapidly evolving landscape of education and assessment, it's essential for RPL providers to stay up to date with best practices and emerging trends. This involves ongoing research, professional development, and collaboration with industry experts and educational institutions. By staying informed and proactive, RPL providers can incorporate innovative practices and methodologies into their assessment processes, ensuring their relevance and effectiveness.

** Engaging Stakeholders in the Improvement Process:*

Continuous improvement is a collective effort that involves engaging stakeholders at every stage of the process. RPL providers should seek input and involvement from learners, assessors, employers, and regulatory bodies in the identification of improvement opportunities and the co-creation of solutions. By developing a culture of collaboration and shared ownership, RPL providers can harness the collective wisdom and expertise of their stakeholders to drive meaningful change.

** Adapting to Technological Advances:*

Technology plays a pivotal role in shaping the future of RPL, offering opportunities for efficiency, accessibility, and innovation. RPL providers should embrace technological advances and leverage digital tools and platforms to streamline assessment processes, enhance learner support services, and expand access to RPL opportunities. By harnessing the power of technology, RPL providers can stay agile and responsive in a rapidly evolving digital landscape.

** Benchmarking and Quality Assurance:*

Continuous improvement is grounded in benchmarking and quality assurance practices that enable RPL providers to compare their performance against industry standards and benchmarks. By benchmarking against established criteria and best practices, RPL providers can identify areas of strength and areas for improvement, driving targeted quality assurance initiatives. This ongoing cycle of benchmarking and improvement ensures that RPL services consistently meet or exceed expectations.

This means that continuous improvement is an important foundational building block of excellence in recognition of prior learning, driving ongoing refinement and enhancement in assessment practices, policies, and procedures. By embracing feedback, regular review, and evaluation, staying informed of best practices, engaging stakeholders, adapting to technological advances, and implementing benchmarking and quality assurance practices, RPL providers can ensure the relevance, effectiveness, and quality of their services, ultimately enhancing learner outcomes and promoting lifelong learning and professional development.

Chapter 22

Implementing Cost-Effective RPL Practices

Introduction:

Types of Evidence Accepted for RPL Assessment

When we discuss implementing cost-effective practices in recognition of prior learning (RPL), it is crucial to understand the types of evidence accepted for RPL assessment. Evidence is at the heart of the RPL process, serving as the foundation upon which recognition decisions are made. In this chapter, we explore the various types of evidence that RPL providers accept and evaluate, empowering learners to showcase their prior learning and skills effectively.

Understanding the Diversity of Evidence:

RPL recognizes that learning takes place in diverse settings and contexts, beyond traditional classroom environments. As such, RPL providers accept a wide range of evidence that reflects this diversity. From work experience and certificates to volunteer work and personal projects, learners can draw upon various forms of evidence to demonstrate their competencies and achievements.

Examples of Permissible Evidence:

Permissible evidence in RPL assessment includes a wide variety of experiences, achievements, and credentials. Work experience provides valuable insights into an individual's skills, knowledge, and capabilities gained through professional practice. Certificates and qualifications validate formal learning achievements, while volunteer work and personal projects demonstrate initiative, creativity, and community engagement.

** Guidelines for Documenting Evidence Effectively:*
Effectively documenting evidence is essential to its recognition and evaluation in the RPL process. RPL providers should provide clear guidelines and instructions to learners on how to document their evidence, ensuring that it aligns with assessment criteria and expectations. Documentation may include resumes, portfolios, written reflections, testimonials, and samples of work, among other forms of evidence.

We work through the detail of cost-effective RPL practices, and find that understanding the types of evidence accepted for assessment lays the groundwork for efficient and equitable recognition processes. By empowering learners to gather and present their evidence effectively, RPL providers can facilitate smoother assessment processes while upholding the integrity and rigor of recognition decisions.

In the remaining sections of this chapter, we will explore strategies for minimizing costs, leveraging technology, and collaborating with industry partners to optimize RPL practices.

Strategies for Minimizing Costs in RPL Assessment

Cost is often a significant consideration in the implementation of recognition of prior learning (RPL) programs. However, it is essential to balance cost-effectiveness with the quality and integrity of the assessment process. In this section, we'll explore various strategies for minimizing costs in RPL assessment without compromising on the fairness or rigor of the process.

** Streamlining Assessment Processes:*

One of the most effective ways to minimize costs in RPL assessment is by streamlining assessment processes. This involves reviewing and optimizing each step of the assessment journey to eliminate ineffectiveness and repetition. By standardizing procedures, reducing administrative overhead, and automating routine tasks where possible, RPL providers can save both time and resources.

** Implementing Scalable Assessment Models:*

Scalability is key to cost-effective RPL assessment. Implementing scalable assessment models allows RPL providers to accommodate varying volumes of assessment requests without significantly increasing costs. Modular assessment frameworks, where learners can demonstrate competency in discrete units or modules, offer flexibility and scalability, enabling providers to tailor assessments to individual needs while managing costs effectively.

** Leveraging Prior Learning Assessment Portfolios:*

Prior learning assessment (PLA) portfolios offer a cost-effective way for learners to document and present their prior learning experiences and achievements. By providing clear guidelines and templates for portfolio development, RPL providers can empower learners to compile and organize their evidence professionally. Additionally, PLA portfolios facilitate self-assessment and reflection, enabling learners to identify gaps in their knowledge and skills before undergoing formal assessment.

** Offering Blended Assessment Options:*

Blended assessment options, which combine traditional assessment methods with technology-enhanced approaches, can help minimize costs while enhancing the assessment experience. For example, incorporating online self-assessment tools, virtual simulations, or peer-reviewed assessments can reduce the need for costly in-person evaluations without compromising assessment quality. Blended approaches also offer greater flexibility for learners, allowing them to engage in assessment activities at their own pace and convenience.

** Embracing Open Educational Resources (OERs):*

Open educational resources (O.E.R.'s) are freely accessible educational materials that can be used, adapted, and shared for teaching, learning, and assessment purposes. By leveraging O.E.R.'s, RPL providers can reduce the costs associated with developing and delivering assessment content. O.E. R.'s include a wide range of resources, such as textbooks, videos, interactive simulations, and assessment tools, which can enhance the quality and diversity of assessment materials while minimizing costs.

** Implementing Efficient Feedback Mechanisms:*

Providing timely and constructive feedback to learners is essential for their growth and development, but it can also be resource intensive. Implementing efficient feedback mechanisms, like:

* Automated feedback systems,
* Peer feedback, or
* Group feedback sessions,

can help reduce the time and effort required to provide feedback while maintaining its effectiveness. By using technology and collaborative learning approaches, RPL providers can streamline the feedback process and minimize costs associated with manual grading and evaluation.

Implementing cost-effective RPL practices requires a strategic approach that balances affordability with quality and integrity.
   By:
   * Streamlining assessment processes,
   * Implementing scalable assessment models,
   * Using P.L.A. portfolios,
   * Offering blended assessment options,
   * Embracing O.E.R's,
   * Implementing efficient feedback mechanisms,

RPL providers can minimize costs while ensuring a fair, rigorous, and inclusive assessment experience for learners. These strategies not only reduce financial burdens but also contribute to the sustainability and scalability of RPL programs, ultimately enhancing access to education and employment opportunities for all learners.

Using Technology for Efficient Assessment Processes

In the fast-paced digital era, technology has become an indispensable tool in various aspects of our lives, including education and assessment. When it comes to recognition of prior learning (RPL), leveraging technology can significantly enhance the efficiency, accessibility, and effectiveness of assessment processes. In this section, we'll explore how RPL providers can harness the power of technology to streamline assessment processes and maximize resources.

1. Digital Portfolios and Online Platforms:

One of the most powerful tools in modern RPL assessment is the digital portfolio. Digital portfolios allow learners to compile and showcase evidence of their prior learning in a convenient and accessible format. RPL providers can use online platforms and tools specifically designed for digital portfolios, offering learners a centralized space to upload, organize, and present their evidence. These platforms often come equipped with features like multimedia support, collaboration tools, and customizable templates, facilitating a seamless and engaging assessment experience.

2. E-Assessment Tools and Platforms:

E-assessment tools and platforms offer RPL providers a range of options for conducting assessments efficiently and securely. These tools enable the creation and administration of various assessment formats, including multiple-choice quizzes, written assignments, and practical demonstrations. E-assessment platforms often feature automated grading functionalities, instant feedback mechanisms, and data analytics capabilities, allowing assessors to evaluate learner performance quickly and accurately. Additionally, e-assessment tools reduce administrative overhead, streamline assessment workflows, and ensure consistency and fairness in evaluation processes.

3. Virtual Assessment Centres and Simulations:

Virtual assessment centres and simulations provide interactive environments for conducting practical assessments in RPL. Through virtual simulations, learners can demonstrate their skills and competencies in realistic scenarios without the need for physical resources or facilities. Virtual assessment centres offer a range of benefits, including flexibility in scheduling, scalability, and cost-effectiveness. By simulating real-world contexts and scenarios, virtual assessments enable assessors to evaluate learners' practical abilities comprehensively while minimizing logistical challenges and resource constraints.

4. Online Collaboration and Communication Tools:

Effective communication and co-operation are essential components of successful RPL assessment processes.

Online participation and communication tools, such as:

* Video conferencing platforms,

* Instant messaging applications,

* Collective document editors,

facilitate seamless interaction and engagement between learners, assessors, and support staff. These tools enable real-time communication, file sharing, and collaborative workspaces, fostering a collaborative learning environment and enhancing learner support services.

5. Data Analytics and Reporting Tools:

Data analytics and reporting tools provide RPL providers with valuable insights into assessment outcomes, learner performance, and process efficiency. By analysing assessment data, RPL providers can identify trends, patterns, and areas for improvement, enabling informed decision-making and targeted interventions. Data analytics tools offer features such as customizable dashboards, predictive analytics, and automated reporting, empowering RPL providers to track progress, measure impact, and optimize assessment processes continually.

Technology offers immense potential for enhancing the efficiency, accessibility, and effectiveness of RPL assessment processes. By embracing digital tools and platforms, RPL providers can streamline assessment workflows, enhance learner engagement, and optimize resource utilization, ultimately delivering high-quality and cost-effective assessment services. As we navigate the evolving landscape of RPL, leveraging technology will be crucial in advancing the field and ensuring equitable access to recognition opportunities for all learners.

Collaborating with Industry Partners for Resource Sharing

In recognition of prior learning (RPL), co-operation with industry partners can be a game-changer. By building partnerships with employers, professional associations, and other stakeholders, RPL providers can have access to a wealth of resources, expertise, and opportunities that can significantly enhance the efficiency and effectiveness of assessment processes.

In this section, we'll explore the benefits of collaborating with industry partners for resource sharing and how RPL providers can leverage these partnerships to optimize their practices.

1. Access to Industry Expertise and Insights:

One of the primary advantages of collaborating with industry partners is gaining access to their expertise and insights. Employers and industry professionals possess valuable knowledge about industry standards, trends, and requirements, which can inform the development of assessment criteria and standards. By involving industry representatives in the assessment process, RPL providers can ensure that assessments are relevant, up-to-date, and aligned with industry needs, ultimately enhancing the credibility and value of RPL outcomes.

2. Sharing of Training Materials and Resources:

Industry partners often have access to a wide range of training materials, resources, and tools that can support RPL assessment processes. From training manuals and instructional videos to simulation software and equipment, these resources can be invaluable in facilitating practical assessments and skills demonstrations. By co-operating with industry partners, RPL providers can access these resources at reduced or no cost, minimizing expenses associated with developing and sourcing assessment materials internally.

3. Work-Based Assessment Opportunities:

Co-operation with industry partners can create opportunities for work-based assessments, where learners can demonstrate their skills and competencies in real-world settings. Employers can provide access to workplace environments, projects, and tasks that serve as authentic assessment contexts for RPL candidates. Work-based assessments offer numerous benefits, including the opportunity for learners to apply their skills in authentic contexts, receive feedback from industry professionals, and gain valuable work experience while undergoing assessment.

4. Industry Validation and Recognition:

Partnering with industry stakeholders can enhance the credibility and recognition of RPL outcomes within the broader professional community. When industry partners endorse RPL assessments and recognize the competencies demonstrated by learners, it enhances the value and relevance of RPL qualifications in the eyes of employers, professional associations, and other stakeholders. Industry validation can lead to increased acceptance of RPL outcomes in the job market and better integration of RPL into workforce development initiatives.

5. Collaborative Program Development:

Industry partnerships can also facilitate collaborative program development, where RPL providers work closely with industry stakeholders to design and deliver customized RPL programs that meet industry needs. By aligning program curricula with industry standards and requirements, RPL providers can ensure that learners develop relevant skills and competencies that are in demand in the labour market. Collaborative program development fosters mutual understanding and engagement between RPL providers and industry partners, leading to more effective and responsive RPL offerings.

Working together with industry partners for resource sharing can yield significant benefits for RPL providers and learners alike. By leveraging industry expertise, accessing training materials and resources, offering work-based assessment opportunities, gaining industry validation, and engaging in collaborative program development, RPL providers can enhance the quality, relevance, and accessibility of their assessment processes, ultimately contributing to the advancement of cost-effective RPL practices and the promotion of lifelong learning and skills development.

Chapter 23

Case Studies and Success Stories

In this chapter, we look at real-life success stories and case studies in recognition of prior learning (RPL).

We will explore inspiring examples of individuals who have embarked on the RPL journey and achieved remarkable success, demonstrating the transformative power of recognizing prior learning experiences. Through these case studies, we will uncover the diverse pathways, challenges overcome, and triumphs celebrated by learners who have undergone RPL assessments.

From seasoned professionals seeking to formalize their skills to individuals returning to education after a break, each case study offers valuable insights into the RPL process and its impact on learners' lives and careers. By sharing these stories, we aim to highlight the tangible benefits of RPL, from accelerated qualification pathways to enhanced employability and career advancement opportunities.

We will also analyse the lessons learned, and best practices collected from these case studies, refining key takeaways that can inform and inspire RPL practitioners, educators, and learners alike. By examining successful RPL experiences from various perspectives and contexts, we'll uncover strategies for optimizing RPL processes, addressing challenges, and maximizing the benefits for all stakeholders involved.

On this journey, we celebrate the achievements of learners who have embraced the RPL pathway, showcasing the transformative potential of recognizing and valuing prior learning experiences. Through these inspiring case studies, we'll reaffirm the importance of RPL in unlocking opportunities, empowering individuals, and promoting lifelong learning and skills development.

Case Studies and Success Stories

Real-life examples of successful RPL experiences serve as powerful testimonials to the effectiveness and impact of recognition of prior learning (RPL) practices. We investigate the stories of individuals who have completed the RPL journey, showcasing their accomplishments, challenges they have overcome, and the transformative outcomes experienced.

Sarah is a seasoned professional in the field of project management. Despite years of hands-on experience and demonstrated expertise, Sarah lacked a formal qualification in her field. Recognizing the value of her practical knowledge, she decided to pursue RPL to attain a recognized certification. Through a comprehensive assessment process that included portfolio submission, skills demonstration, and competency interviews, Sarah successfully obtained her project management qualification. RPL not only validated her existing skills but also provided her with a pathway to career advancement and enhanced credibility within her industry.

Alex, a skilled tradesperson with years of on-the-job experience in carpentry, was faced with the prospect of obtaining formal certification to progress in his career. He used RPL for a solution. Through a thorough assessment process that evaluated his practical skills and knowledge, Alex achieved recognition for his expertise, earning his certification without the need for additional training or classroom instruction. RPL not only saved Alex time and money but also provided him with the validation and confidence to pursue higher-level opportunities in his field.

These are just two examples of the countless success stories that illustrate the transformative potential of RPL. From professionals seeking to formalize their skills to individuals re-entering the workforce or changing careers, RPL offers a flexible and accessible pathway to recognition and qualification attainment. So, we look at some more examples from various fields.

Profiles of learners who benefited from RPL

Each profile will highlight the individual's background, motivations for pursuing RPL, the assessment process undertaken, and the outcomes achieved. Through these personal accounts, readers will gain insight into the diverse pathways and experiences of RPL participants, showcasing the breadth of opportunities and benefits afforded by the RPL process.

Lessons learned and best practices from case studies:

When we analyse common themes, challenges, and success factors across various RPL experiences, we notice valuable insights that can inform and enhance RPL practices. Whether it is optimizing assessment processes, providing tailored support to learners, or building partnerships with industry stakeholders, these lessons will serve as a guide for RPL practitioners and educators striving to create impactful and effective recognition pathways for learners.

Profiles of Learners Who Benefited from RPL:
  **Emily: Stay-at-Home Mom to Certified Nurse:*
Emily is a dedicated mother who spent years raising her children, before deciding to pursue her life-long dream of becoming a nurse. Despite lacking formal education in the field, Emily possessed valuable caregiving skills and experiences gained from caring for her family. Through RPL, Emily was able to demonstrate her practical skills, knowledge, and compassion, earning recognition for her prior learning and securing a place in a nursing program. Today, Emily works as a certified nurse, fulfilling her passion for helping others and serving as an inspiration to fellow learners.

**Mark's Career Advancement Through RPL in Information Technology:*
Mark, an IT professional with years of industry experience but no formal qualifications, faced barriers to career progression due to the lack of recognized credentials. Determined to advance his career, Mark pursued RPL to validate his skills and knowledge. Through a comprehensive assessment process, Mark demonstrated his proficiency in various IT domains, earning recognition for his expertise and securing promotions within his organization. RPL not only accelerated Mark's career but also boosted his confidence and credibility in the workplace.

**Maria's Transition from Military Service to Civilian Employment:*
Maria, a military veteran transitioning to civilian life, encountered challenges in translating her military experience into civilian qualifications. With RPL, Maria was able to leverage her military training and skills to gain recognition for relevant certifications and

credentials. Through tailored assessment processes designed to recognize military experience, Maria successfully transitioned to a fulfilling career in the civilian workforce, equipped with the qualifications and confidence to thrive in her new role.

Carlos' Entrepreneurial Success Through RPL in Business Management:
    Carlos, an aspiring entrepreneur with a talent for business, sought to formalize his skills and knowledge in business management. Despite lacking formal education, Carlos possessed years of hands-on experience running his own small business. Through RPL, Carlos was able to demonstrate his entrepreneurial expertise, strategic thinking, and leadership skills, earning recognition for his prior learning and achieving a formal qualification in business management. Today, Carlos's business thrives, thanks to the practical insights and knowledge gained through the RPL process.

These profiles represent just a few examples of the diverse learners who have benefited from RPL. Their stories highlight the transformative potential of recognizing and validating prior learning, enabling individuals to overcome barriers, achieve their goals, and embark on new opportunities.

Lessons Learned and Best Practices from Case Studies

The case studies presented in this chapter offer valuable lessons and best practices that can inform and enhance RPL practices:

Tailored Assessment Processes:

One size does not fit all when it comes to RPL assessment. The case studies highlight the importance of tailoring assessment processes to suit the individual needs and circumstances of learners. By offering flexibility in assessment methods and recognizing diverse forms of evidence, RPL providers can ensure fair and equitable outcomes for all learners.

Comprehensive Support Services:

Effective RPL programs provide comprehensive support services to guide learners through the assessment process. From initial guidance and information sessions to ongoing mentorship and feedback, personalized support can help learners navigate the complexities of RPL and maximize their chances of success.

Collaboration and Partnerships:

Collaborating with industry partners and stakeholders is crucial for enhancing the relevance and currency of RPL assessments. By engaging employers, industry bodies, and other relevant stakeholders, RPL providers can ensure that assessments align with industry standards and meet the evolving needs of the workforce.

Continuous Improvement:

RPL is a repetitive process that requires ongoing evaluation and refinement. By obtaining feedback from learners, assessors, and other stakeholders, RPL providers can identify areas for improvement and implement changes to enhance the quality and effectiveness of their programs.

These case studies and success stories presented in this chapter demonstrates the transformative potential of RPL and offer valuable insights into the best practices that make successful RPL possible. When we combine a tailored assessment process, comprehensive support services, collaboration with industry partners, and a commitment to continuous improvement, RPL providers can empower learners to achieve their goals of obtaining a formal qualification though RPL.

Chapter 24

Future Trends and Innovations in RPL

In this chapter, we discuss the exciting possibilities in the future of RPL, and discuss how RPL practices are ready to evolve in response to changing educational paradigms and technological advancements.

Emerging trends in RPL assessment methods

The traditional methods of RPL assessment, such as portfolio submission and skills demonstration, have long been the basis of recognition processes. However, we are witnessing a shift towards more innovative and flexible assessment methods. From competency-based assessments to experiential learning portfolios, RPL providers are exploring new ways to evaluate learners' prior knowledge and skills accurately and holistically.

Potential impact of technology and automation

Technology is transforming every aspect of education, and RPL is no exception. The integration of digital platforms, data analytics, and artificial intelligence presents exciting opportunities to streamline assessment processes, enhance the accessibility of RPL services, and provide personalized learning pathways for learners. Additionally, automation tools can help reduce administrative burdens, allowing assessors to focus more on meaningful interactions with learners.

Opportunities for enhancing RPL practices in the future.

There are numerous new opportunities for enhancing RPL practices to better serve learners and meet the evolving needs of the workforce. Collaboration between education providers, industry stakeholders, and government agencies can facilitate the development of standardized RPL frameworks and credentialing systems. Also, investments in professional development for assessors and the establishment of quality assurance mechanisms can ensure the integrity and consistency of RPL assessments.

By embracing emerging trends, leveraging technological innovations, and building co-operation, we can create a future where RPL serves as an inspiration for lifelong learning and empowers individuals to unlock their full potential.

We must remain steadfast in our commitment to empowering learners through the recognition of their prior learning experiences.

We must consider the exciting developments and innovations that are reshaping the landscape of assessment practices. As we investigate the emerging trends, we will see how technology, partnership, and modern strategies are driving the evolution of RPL and empowering learners to achieve their educational and career goals.

Emerging Trends in RPL Assessment Methods

Traditionally, RPL assessment methods have relied on portfolio submissions, interviews, and skills demonstrations to evaluate learners' prior knowledge and skills. However, we're witnessing a paradigm shift towards more flexible and innovative assessment approaches. Competency-based assessments, for example, focus on measuring learners' ability to perform specific tasks and achieve predefined learning outcomes, rather than solely relying on formal qualifications or credentials.

Experiential learning portfolios are another emerging trend in RPL assessment. These portfolios allow learners to showcase their skills, knowledge, and achievements gained through real-world experiences such as work, volunteering, or personal projects. By providing a comprehensive overview of learners' capabilities, experiential learning portfolios offer an all-inclusive and refined assessment of their prior learning.

Simulation-based assessments are also gaining popularity in RPL, particularly in fields where practical skills are of greatest importance, such as healthcare, engineering, and trades. These assessments involve simulated scenarios or tasks designed to replicate real-world situations, allowing learners to demonstrate their competency in a controlled environment.

Furthermore, digital badges and micro-credentials are becoming increasingly popular as a means of recognizing and validating specific skills and competencies acquired through informal or non-traditional learning experiences. These portable credentials provide learners with tangible evidence of their achievements, enhancing their employability and professional development opportunities.

Overall, the emergence of these innovative assessment methods reflects a growing recognition of the diverse ways in which individuals acquire knowledge and skills outside of formal educational settings. By embracing these trends, RPL practitioners can offer more inclusive, flexible, and equitable assessment processes that truly reflect learners' capabilities and experiences.

Potential Impact of Technology and Automation

Technology and automation are composed to revolutionize RPL assessment practices, offering new opportunities to streamline processes, enhance accessibility, and improve the overall assessment experience for learners and assessors alike.

One significant impact of technology on RPL is the digitization of assessment processes. Digital platforms and online portfolios enable learners to submit evidence of their prior learning electronically, reducing the administrative burden associated with paper-based assessments and facilitating more efficient feedback and review processes.

Moreover, the integration of data analytics and artificial intelligence (AI) in RPL assessment holds great promise for personalized learning experiences and adaptive assessment strategies. AI-powered algorithms can analyse large datasets of learner performance and behaviour to identify patterns, trends, and areas for improvement, enabling assessors to provide targeted support and interventions tailored to individual learners' needs.

Automation tools, such as machine learning algorithms and natural language processing, can also assist in the assessment of digital artifacts and portfolios, automating tasks such as plagiarism detection, content analysis, and competency mapping. By automating routine tasks, assessors can focus their time and expertise on more meaningful aspects of the assessment process, such as providing personalized feedback and guidance to learners.

Additionally, technology-enabled assessment tools, such as virtual reality simulations and interactive multimedia platforms, offer immersive and engaging learning experiences that closely simulate real-world contexts. These tools allow learners to practice and demonstrate their skills in a risk-free environment, enhancing their confidence and competence in their chosen field.

Overall, the potential impact of technology and automation on RPL assessment is vast, offering opportunities to enhance efficiency, effectiveness, and equity in assessment processes while ensuring the validity and reliability of assessment outcomes.

** Opportunities for Enhancing RPL Practices in the Future*
In future, there are numerous opportunities for enhancing RPL practices to better meet the needs of learners, employers, and society. Co-operation between educational institutions, industry partners, government agencies, and other stakeholders is essential to developing and implementing standardized RPL frameworks, assessment tools, and credentialing systems.

Investments in professional development for RPL practitioners are also crucial to ensuring the quality and consistency of assessment processes. Training programs, workshops, and peer networks can provide assessors with the knowledge, skills, and resources they need to effectively assess learners' prior learning and provide meaningful feedback and support.

In addition, research and innovation in RPL assessment are essential for advancing the field and addressing emerging challenges and opportunities. Interdisciplinary research collaborations, pilot projects, and continued studies, can help identify best practices, evaluate the effectiveness of assessment methods, and inform policy decisions to support the continued growth and evolution of RPL.

The future of RPL is filled with promise and potential. Emerging trends such as competency-based assessments, digital portfolios, and simulation-based learning, offer new pathways for learners to demonstrate their skills and knowledge and achieve their educational and career goals. Technology and automation hold the power to transform assessment practices, making assessment processes more efficient, accessible, and personalized. Co-operation, teamwork, partnerships, innovation, and a commitment to lifelong learning, are essential for realizing the full benefits of RPL and empowering learners to thrive in an ever-changing world. As we continue to explore and embrace these future trends and innovations, let us remain steadfast in our dedication to empowering learners through the recognition of their prior learning experiences.

As we face the future of recognition of prior learning (RPL), it is impossible to ignore the great impact that technology and automation have on assessment practices.

What are the potential implications of these advancements, if we consider both the opportunities it present and the challenges it may involve?

Potential Impact of Technology and Automation

Technology has already begun to revolutionize various aspects of RPL assessment, from the way evidence is collected and evaluated to the methods used for providing feedback and support to learners. As we continue to embrace technological innovations, several key areas stand out in terms of their potential impact on RPL practices:

** Enhanced Efficiency:*

One of the most significant benefits of technology in RPL assessment is the potential to streamline processes and reduce administrative burdens. Digital platforms and online assessment tools enable learners to submit evidence electronically, eliminating the need for paper-based submissions and manual data entry. Automation can also play a crucial role in automating routine tasks, such as plagiarism detection and content analysis, allowing assessors to focus their time and expertise on more value-added activities.

** Improved Accessibility:*

Technology has the power to make RPL assessment more accessible and inclusive for learners from diverse backgrounds. Online assessment platforms can accommodate learners with disabilities by providing alternative formats and customizable settings. Additionally, the flexibility of digital assessment tools allows learners to complete assessments at their own pace and convenience, overcoming barriers such as geographical distance and scheduling constraints.

** Personalized Learning Experiences:*

Technology-enabled assessment tools, such as adaptive learning algorithms and personalized feedback systems, have the potential to provide learners with tailored learning experiences. By analysing learners' performance data and preferences, these tools can deliver targeted support and interventions, helping learners identify areas for improvement and pursue their educational goals more effectively.

Data-Driven Decision Making:

The use of data analytics and artificial intelligence (AI) in RPL assessment can provide valuable insights into learners' progress, preferences, and learning outcomes. By analysing large datasets of learner performance, AI-powered algorithms can identify patterns, trends, and connections that inform decision making and drive continuous improvement in assessment practices.

Enhanced Security and Integrity:

Technology can also play a crucial role in ensuring the security and integrity of RPL assessments. Blockchain technology, for example, offers a tamper-proof and transparent record of assessment outcomes, providing reassurance to both learners and stakeholders about the authenticity and validity of credentials.

However, along with these opportunities, the widespread adoption of technology and automation in RPL assessment also raises important considerations and challenges. Privacy concerns, data security risks, digital divide issues, and ethical implications, are just a few of the factors that must be carefully navigated to ensure that technology enhances rather than weakens the integrity and effectiveness of RPL practices.

As we continue to explore the potential impact of technology and automation on RPL assessment, it is essential to approach these advancements with a critical eye and a commitment to ethical, inclusive, and learner-cantered practices. By leveraging technology thoughtfully and responsibly, we can unlock new possibilities for empowering learners through the recognition of their prior learning experiences.

As we look deeper into the future of Recognition of Prior Learning (RPL), it is crucial to consider the opportunities that lie ahead for enhancing RPL practices.

We continue to explore the potential pathways to advance RPL methods, ensuring they remain relevant, accessible, and effective in recognizing learners' prior experiences and competencies.

Embracing Technological Advancements:

One of the most promising avenues for enhancing RPL practices lies in leveraging technological advancements. With the rapid evolution of digital tools and platforms, there is a vast potential to streamline and optimize the RPL process. Integrating online platforms for evidence submission, assessment, and feedback can significantly improve efficiency and accessibility for both learners and assessors. Additionally, the integration of artificial intelligence (AI) and machine learning algorithms holds promise in automating certain aspects of the assessment process, making it more scalable and standardized.

Personalized Learning Pathways:

In the future, we envision a shift towards more personalized learning pathways driven by RPL. By utilizing data analytics and learner profiling techniques, RPL providers can tailor learning experiences to individual needs and competencies identified through the RPL process. This approach not only enhances learner engagement and motivation but also maximizes the value of prior learning experiences by seamlessly integrating them into ongoing educational journeys.

Enhanced Collaboration and Recognition:

Collaboration among educational institutions, industries, and accrediting bodies presents an opportunity to enhance the recognition and portability of RPL outcomes. By establishing common standards, frameworks, and credit transfer mechanisms, learners can seamlessly transition between educational pathways and employment sectors, maximizing the value of their prior learning achievements. Moreover, fostering partnerships with employers can lead to the development of industry-validated competency frameworks, ensuring that RPL outcomes align with current and future workforce needs.

Accessible and Inclusive RPL Practices:

It is important to prioritize accessibility and inclusivity in RPL practices. This involves removing barriers to participation, such as language, cultural, or socioeconomic factors, and ensuring that RPL processes are equitable and transparent for all learners. Adopting innovative assessment methods, such as micro-credentials, digital badges, and competency-based assessments, can provide more flexible and accessible pathways for recognizing diverse forms of prior learning.

Chapter 25

Empowering Learners
through Recognition of Prior Learning

Recap of Key Concepts and Strategies

As we come to the end of our journey through the world of Recognition of Prior Learning (RPL), it is essential to take a moment to reflect on the key concepts and strategies we've explored. Throughout this book, we have investigated the significance of RPL in unlocking opportunities for learners, the processes involved, and the ways in which institutions and policymakers can support and promote RPL initiatives.

RPL acknowledges and values the knowledge, skills, and experiences individuals have acquired through various life experiences. Whether gained through work, volunteer activities, or personal interests, this prior learning forms the foundation upon which further learning and development can occur.

One of the fundamental models that we have discussed, is the idea of lifelong learning. RPL uses this concept by providing learners with pathways to further education and career advancement, regardless of their age, background, or previous educational experiences. By recognizing and accrediting prior learning, RPL encourages learners to use learning as a continuous and lifelong pursuit.

Strategies for implementing RPL effectively have also been a focal point of our discussion. We have explored the importance of clear assessment criteria, robust evidence-gathering processes, and effective communication between learners, assessors, and institutions. Additionally, we've highlighted the role of technology in streamlining RPL processes, making them more accessible and efficient for all stakeholders involved.

Furthermore, we have emphasized the need for co-operation and partnership between educational institutions, employers, industry organizations, and policymakers, to ensure that RPL is integrated into broader education and workforce development initiatives. By working together, we can create a more seamless and supportive environment for learners seeking recognition of their prior learning.

Encouragement for Learners to Pursue RPL Opportunities

As we promote and encourage the advantages of Recognition of Prior Learning (RPL), it is important to encourage learners to welcome the opportunities RPL presents. Throughout this book, we have discussed how RPL can be a transformative journey, unlocking doors to education, career advancement, and personal growth for individuals from all walks of life.

I want to address all learners who may be considering pursuing RPL opportunities. Whether you are a working professional seeking to validate your skills and experiences, a returning student looking to accelerate your educational journey, or someone seeking to re-enter the workforce, RPL offers you a pathway to recognition and advancement. It's essential to recognize the value of your prior learning and understand that it is a legitimate and worthy foundation upon which to build your future achievements.

One of the key messages I want to convey to learners is the importance of self-advocacy and initiative when pursuing RPL. Take ownership of your learning journey, gather evidence of your skills and experiences, and be proactive in seeking recognition for what you already know and can do. Don't hesitate to reach out to educational institutions, employers, or RPL assessors to explore RPL options and opportunities available to you.

Furthermore, I encourage learners to approach RPL with an open mind and a willingness to learn. RPL is not just about obtaining credentials; it's about reflecting on your experiences, identifying your strengths and areas for development, and leveraging your prior learning to set new goals and aspirations. Embrace the opportunity to engage in reflective practice, self-assessment, and lifelong learning as integral parts of the RPL process.

Additionally, I want to emphasize the importance of persistence and resilience. The RPL journey may not always be straightforward, and you may encounter challenges along the way. But remember that every obstacle is an opportunity for growth, and every setback is a chance to learn and improve. Stay committed to your goals, stay resilient in the face of adversity, and never underestimate the power of your own potential.

Finally, I want to remind learners that RPL is not just about individual achievement; it's also about contributing to a larger collective goal of promoting lifelong learning and fostering a culture of recognition and respect for diverse forms of knowledge and expertise. By pursuing RPL opportunities, you are not only investing in your own future but also contributing to a more inclusive and equitable society where everyone's talents and contributions are valued and celebrated.

I urge all learners to seize the opportunities presented by RPL, to embrace the journey of self-discovery and empowerment it offers, and to start on a lifelong path of learning, growth, and fulfilment. The possibilities are endless, and the journey is yours to explore. Embrace it with courage, determination, and an unwavering belief in your own potential.

Call to Action for Institutions and Policymakers to Support RPL Initiatives

As we conclude this book on Recognition of Prior Learning (RPL), it is essential to recognize the vital role that institutions and policymakers play in shaping the landscape of RPL and building an environment where learners can truly benefit from its potential. In this final chapter, we issue a call to action for institutions and policymakers to actively support and promote RPL initiatives, thereby empowering learners and advancing educational equity and access.

Institutions, including educational providers, employers, and industry organizations, must recognize the value of RPL as a tool for promoting lifelong learning and enhancing workforce development. They should prioritize the integration of RPL into their educational and training programs, ensuring that learners have opportunities to receive credit for their prior learning experiences. This requires a commitment to developing robust RPL policies and procedures, providing adequate resources and support for RPL assessors and coordinators, and raising awareness among learners about the benefits of RPL.

Furthermore, institutions should strive to make the RPL process as accessible and transparent as possible, removing barriers to participation and ensuring that all learners, regardless of their background or circumstances, have equitable access to RPL opportunities. This may involve offering flexible assessment methods, providing guidance and support to learners throughout the RPL process, and addressing any systemic biases or inequalities that may exist within the RPL framework.

In addition to institutional support, policymakers play an important role in advancing RPL initiatives at the national, regional, and local levels. They should recognize RPL as a key component of educational and workforce development policy and allocate adequate funding and resources to support its implementation and expansion. Policymakers should also work to create a supportive policy environment for RPL, including legislation that promotes the recognition and transferability of RPL credits, motivates institutions to participate in RPL programs, and encourages collaboration between education providers, employers, and other stakeholders.

Policymakers should prioritize initiatives aimed at raising awareness about RPL among learners, employers, and educational institutions, highlighting its benefits and encouraging its uptake. This may involve launching public awareness campaigns, distributing information about RPL opportunities through various channels, and partnering with stakeholders to promote RPL as a viable pathway to education and employment.

Ultimately, the success of RPL initiatives depends on the collective efforts of institutions, policymakers, educators, employers, and learners themselves. By working together to promote RPL, and create an enabling environment for its implementation, we can unlock the full potential of learners, empower individuals to achieve their educational and career goals, and build a more inclusive and equitable society where everyone can succeed and prosper.

In conclusion, we call on institutions and policymakers to embrace RPL as a powerful tool for promoting lifelong learning, promoting workforce development, and advancing educational equity and access. By investing in RPL initiatives and creating supportive policy environments, we can ensure that all learners can receive recognition for their prior learning experiences and realize their full potential. Together, let's empower learners through recognition of prior learning and pave the way for a brighter and more equitable future for all.

Don't miss out!

Visit the website below and you can sign up to receive emails whenever Dr. Francois Meyer (D'Th, DD, PhD) publishes a new book. There's no charge and no obligation.

https://books2read.com/r/B-A-PJOIB-RSODD

BOOKS 2 READ

Connecting independent readers to independent writers.

About the Author

I am an Internationally Ordained Minister, Certified & Ordained Life Coach Minister, Qualified Pastoral Counsellor, Cognitive Behavioral Therapy Practitioner, and Criminal Psychology & Behavioral Analysis Practitioner.

All my courses are produced after careful and extensive research in the specific field, providing you with updated facts and information to help you prosper in your field.

I specialize in Adult Education for 30 years, and Counselling in fields like adult learning, psychology, counselling, positive enhancement skills, criminal behaviour, etc. and my PhD major is theology and pastoral counselling.

I specialize in Adult Education, Mentoring and Counselling, and as a professional coach, I inspire, mentor, train and coach ordained ministers, life coaches, counsellors, law enforcement officers, emergency personnel, and teachers, etc. to reach NEW HEIGHTS in their careers and personal lives.

I provide Counselling, Life Coaching and Mentoring to Teachers, Trainers, and Instructors, and Life Coaching to Law Enforcement Officers, Military Vets (including Private Sector Security), and Emergency Personnel around the world. It may also include spiritual counselling and guidance if required.

By doing so, I also worked with a diversity of ethical, ethnical and language groups, often reaching the proverbial "glass ceiling" with students. These will refer to language barriers, environmental barriers, etc.

I break the ceiling, so you can fly right through. During the entire period of 30+ years, I have experienced a broad spectrum of human nature and dealt with different ethical, religious, and ethnical groups, hereby realizing the shortfall in effective communication, positive attitude, and commitment.

I realized that by assisting individuals in recognizing such shortfalls and turning this into a positive mindset, amazing results could be achieved, whether at work, home or anywhere else.

I constantly do extensive research on all products to ensure that products remain up to date with latest trends and daily life.

I will always remain professional and reliable, providing all clients with ethical and humanitarian practice, yet meeting all present and future demands in a cost-effective manner.

-Dr Francois Meyer-

Read more at https://ecoursez.com/.